SHEER
YVES
SAINT
LAURENT

This book accompanies the exhibition Yves Saint Laurent: Transparences, *presented at the Cité de la Dentelle et de la Mode, Calais, from 24 June to 12 November 2023, then at the Musée Yves Saint Laurent Paris, from 9 February to 1 September 2024.*

COVER Evening gown worn by Danielle Luquet de Saint Germain, Autumn–Winter 1968–1969 haute couture collection. Photograph by Peter Caine.

PP. 1–8 Evening gown (detail), Autumn–Winter 2000–2001 haute couture collection; evening gown (detail), Spring–Summer 1975 haute couture collection; evening gown (detail), Autumn–Winter 1971–1972 haute couture collection; evening gown (detail), Autumn–Winter 1996–1997 haute couture collection; tuxedo blouse (detail), Spring–Summer 1968 haute couture collection. Photographs by Patricia Canino.

SHEER YVES SAINT LAURENT

T&H

Musée Yves Saint Laurent Paris

Sheer Yves Saint Laurent: how better to sum up the creative genius of this most modern of couturiers? By draping it in sheer, fluid chiffon, Cigaline® and lace, Saint Laurent found a way to show off the female body in all its power and sensuality.

And where better than Calais to present the first phase of this exhibition before it moves to Paris in 2024? Because it makes perfect sense to study Yves Saint Laurent's connection with sheer fabrics in the city whose heart, for over two centuries, has been beating to the rhythm of those formidable cast-iron and steel monuments that create Calais-Caudry® lace – Leavers looms.

The manufacturing secrets of this luxurious fabric remained tucked away in the Calais workshops, with no fewer than fifteen years required to train a worker in tulle. A process of initiation that was not even written down for many years, faithful instead to a tradition of oral transmission, observation and apprenticeship. Today, Calais is involved in training lace-makers on mechanical looms and the city's lace and fashion museum, the Cité de la Dentelle et de la Mode, now houses a lacemaking training centre.

Lace is an exceptional fabric destined for luxury haute couture, ready-to-wear and top-end lingerie creations. We see it paraded along the catwalks of Paris, Milan and New York, gracing the pages of glossy fashion magazines and adorning celebrities and beautifully dressed women across the globe thanks to the talents of the top couturiers. One such couturier is Yves Saint Laurent, who was responsible for transforming the lace made by the Calais ateliers into veritable works of art.

Natacha Bouchart
Mayor of Calais
President of the Communauté d'Agglomération Grand Calais Terres & Mers
Vice-president of the Région Hauts-de-France

Evening gown (detail), Autumn–Winter 1971–1972 haute couture collection.
Cité de la Dentelle et de la Mode collection, Calais. Photograph by Patricia Canino.

When we speak of transparency and all that the word evokes, what often comes to mind is a sense of clarity, etherealness, delicacy and lightness. When the concept of transparency was explored by the late master French couturier Yves Saint Laurent, it became all those things and, at the same time, something of great brilliance and force. As Saint Laurent was frequently quoted as saying, nothing is more beautiful than the naked body; his evocation of the feminine form, in both silhouette and contour, infused his work with a uniquely dual quality of mystery and vitality.

Throughout Saint Laurent's long career, as manifested in his vast creative work, the female body was often draped, cloaked, swathed or wrapped in some of the most extraordinary fabrics ever created, which in turn produced clothing that, while profoundly sensual, empowered the women who wore it, bestowing on them an aura of strength and freedom.

It is a great honour for us to pay tribute to this aspect of Yves Saint Laurent's legacy with this exceptional exhibition, a joint endeavor between the Musée des Beaux-Arts de Calais and the Musée Yves Saint Laurent Paris. I would especially like to thank the scientific committee – Shazia Boucher, curator of heritage and assistant director, and her colleague, Anne-Claire Laronde, head curator and director of the Calais museums – for this unique opportunity to collaborate with the Paris museum. This working relationship between the two institutions has allowed the Musée Yves Saint Laurent Paris to delve deeper into, and enrich its understanding of, the abundant collection of designs that makes the Fondation Pierre Bergé – Yves Saint Laurent a unique institution within the realm of fashion.

The Paris branch of the scientific committee – headed by Elsa Janssen, director of the Musée Yves Saint Laurent Paris, joined by Serena Bucalo-Mussely, head of collections and by Domitille Éblé, head of the graphic arts collections – along with the entire team at the Fondation, have worked tirelessly to produce a masterful and fascinating exhibition. I applaud you all, and on behalf of the Foundation, I thank you for further enriching our understanding of Yves Saint Laurent's forceful vision.

This remarkable collaboration between the Cité de la Dentelle et de la Mode in Calais and the Musée Yves Saint Laurent Paris further underscores the unique position the late couturier still commands within the sphere of fashion. On another level, may this exhibition further a dialogue on the importance of individual expression and interpretation in a time when many of those freedoms are in peril for so many. *Vive la liberté!*

Madison Cox
President of the Fondation Pierre Bergé – Yves Saint Laurent

Evening ensemble worn by Mounia Orosemane during preparations for the Autumn–Winter 1979–1980 haute couture collection, salons at 5 avenue Marceau, Paris, 1979. Photograph by François-Marie Banier.

This book and the two exhibitions that it accompanies, in Calais and Paris, give us new insights into the work of an artist who profoundly influenced his era. For the Cité de la Dentelle et de la Mode in Calais, a museum dedicated to this very special fabric, the project was also an opportunity to study and to showcase its own collection of Yves Saint Laurent creations.

The opportunity to collaborate with the teams from the Musée Yves Saint Laurent Paris, who strive to conserve and perpetuate the memory of the couturier's creations, was particularly valuable in this regard, enabling a new approach to the subject and the exchange of unique sources of knowledge. A whole array of little-known data relating to fabrics, designs and clients has thus been brought into the public domain.

The project is also an opportunity, as I see it, to shine a more contemporary spotlight on the work of Yves Saint Laurent. The product of a multi-person collaboration, the book and the two exhibitions give us a chance to look *behind* the couturier's oeuvre and see it from his point of view, and within the context of his times. By creating transparency that showed off a woman's body, by cutting into clothing in bold and original ways as if he were opening a window onto that body, was Yves Saint Laurent a man of his time striving to liberate women, or was he emphasizing their sensuality? Were his models pawns in a game of seduction, or were they at the forefront of a movement in which women would claim a new position for themselves in late 20th-century society?

Admiring Yves Saint Laurent's clothing is also a *physical* pleasure, and the photographer Patricia Canino invites us to feast our eyes. She delights in showing us the couturier's creations floating free of their wearers to give us a better idea of volume, form and space, and by creating the impression of fleeting movement, she conjures up potential lives for these signature garments.

Anne-Claire Laronde
Chief Heritage Curator
Director of the Musées de la Ville de Calais

Coat (detail), Autumn–Winter 1964–1965 haute couture collection. Cité de la Dentelle et de la Mode collection, Calais. Photograph by Patricia Canino.

Looking at the work of Yves Saint Laurent is an opportunity both to observe the evolution of clothes and to re-read the history of art. It helps us recognize the extent to which artists and sculptors have been inspired by the human body and the garments we wear. Transparency in the creations of Yves Saint Laurent created a scandal in the same way that Italian Renaissance nudes – the work of Donatello or Michelangelo – were to revolutionize Western art.

With Yves Saint Laurent, there were always two driving forces that motivated his work: the will to be bold and to embrace modernity, on the one hand, and on the other a desire to reference, and pay homage to, the great names in fashion and in art. The comments of the model Rebecca Ayoko reveal how, like a sculptor with his muse, the couturier needed to be in the presence of a naked, living body if he was to come up with new creative ideas. As he said himself, 'In order to work and make my dresses, I need a living model.'

To put together an exhibition focusing on transparency and display these garments without a living body, without skin, shoulders, breasts or back, was by definition a real challenge. The fabrics and the cut took centre stage, once again demonstrating the sculptural quality of Yves Saint Laurent's designs. How, by sketching a silhouette, did he manage to seize hold of the material, its opacity or its delicacy, and envision a resolutely modern woman? How, through transparency and sheerness, did he manage to reveal a woman who was both gentle and powerful?

With great finesse, the couturier drew on traditional craftsmanship and techniques – an utterly fascinating aspect of his work which we are delighted to be able to explore in a two-phase exhibition: first in the historic city of Calais, which played an important role in the history of lacemaking, and subsequently in Paris, within the walls of the former couture house at 5 avenue Marceau. The project involved studying the subtleties of lace, chiffon, Cigaline® and tulle as reflected in the garments in our own collection, while also providing a magnificent opportunity to work with the Cité de la Dentelle et de la Mode in Calais, an exceptional museum and a mine of expert information regarding textiles, craftsmanship and fashion.

It also enabled us to take advantage of a most unusual venue, a converted factory and its modern extension, with an exhibition layout incorporating light and shadow, designed by Simon de Tovar and Alain Batifoulier, and featuring photographs – which were also used to illustrate this book – by Patricia Canino.

I particularly wish to thank Anne-Claire Laronde and Shazia Boucher for initiating the project along with Olivier Flaviano, Aurélie Samuel and Lola Fournier and enabling us to immerse ourselves in the infinite richness of lace, in all its technical complexity and transparency. Special thanks are also due to Domitille Éblé for co-curating this exhibition with the teams in Calais, and to all those who have been involved in the realization of this exhibition and this catalogue.

Elsa Janssen
Director of the Musée Yves Saint Laurent Paris

Evening gown worn by Dominique Pommier,
Autumn–Winter 1971–1972 haute couture collection.

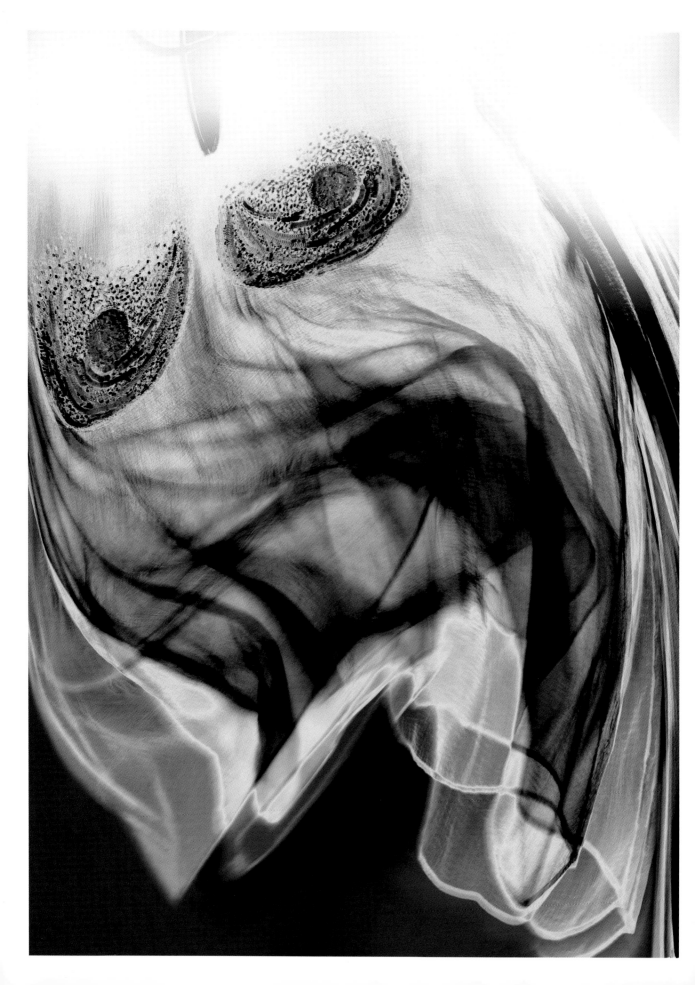

Sheer revelations

When a piece of clothing is transparent enough to reveal part, or parts, of a human body, the eye of the viewer is drawn to the nakedness that is veiled or unveiled, exposed or concealed. The subtlety of sheer fabrics creates a sense of volume, form and contour.

When a piece of clothing is photographed flat, the light plays on the transparent fabric itself: now, the eye is drawn to the fullness of the tulle, the flow of the chiffon, the sculptural effects of the Cigaline®, the lace motifs, whether sequinned, embroidered or iridescent. The textures of these transparent fabrics conjure up the memory of movement. Thanks to the power of light, each arrangement of folds, volumes and forms evokes the life of the garment on the body of the wearer.

Patricia Canino
Photographer

Blouse forming part of an evening ensemble (detail),
SAINT LAURENT *rive gauche* Autumn–Winter 1988–1989
collection. Photograph by Patricia Canino.

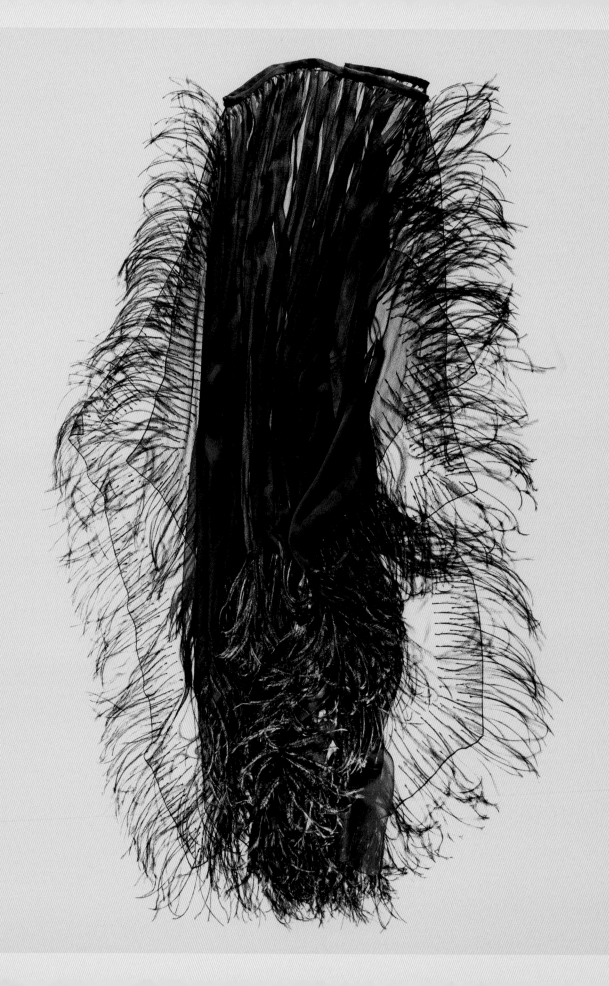

The body laid bare
by the couturier

Émilie Hammen

'Because they share in the perpetually idealizing vision of art, clothes must be seen and studied as paintings are seen and studied – not primarily as cultural by-products or personal expressions but as connected links in a creative tradition of image-making.'[1]

The work of Yves Saint Laurent has attracted a great many commentators, many of whom have eagerly embraced the idea put forward by art historian Anne Hollander, in her famous essay *Seeing Through Clothes*, that clothes are part of the great pictorial tradition and, as such, are worthy of the same analytical approach as the other visual arts. Ample parallels have been drawn between the couturier's designs and modern art across forty years' worth of retrospective writings and exhibitions – from New York's Metropolitan Museum of Art in 1983 to Paris's Centre Pompidou and Musée d'Art Moderne in 2022. Saint Laurent himself encouraged these connections by incorporating motifs from art into his designs, beginning in 1965 with his first Mondrian-inspired dress. In fact, the exercise seems extremely straightforward: this element of the fashion designer's career can virtually be summed up by listing great names from the history of art.

There are two issues with this, however. The first lies in the fact that Yves Saint Laurent and his partner Pierre Bergé regularly argued that fashion and art were not the same, even though, paradoxically, it suited them to believe that the couturier could also be an artist. The second lies in the conceptual weakness of a reading based purely on aesthetic affinities. What do we really learn from the connection between a dress and a painting that look similar? Quotations and appropriations – common as they are in contemporary art – add up to no more than a superficial (albeit satisfying) kind of formal resemblance.[2]

The theme of transparency in the work of Yves Saint Laurent, which is more abstract but no less recurrent than references to art, promises us greater scope. As it gradually appears, reveals itself, shifts and disappears again, transparency invites us to take a closer look at the visual culture within which the couturier was working. Using the tools of his own trade – fabric, cutting, tailoring – he was once again able to enter into a dialogue with the art of his times, perhaps in an even more eloquent fashion than before.

1. Anne Hollander, *Seeing Through Clothes*, New York: Viking Press, 1978, p. xvi.

2. See the analyses by Nancy Troy, notably those in *Couture Culture: A Study of Modern Art and Fashion*, Cambridge, MA: MIT Press, 2003.

ILL. 1 Evening ensemble worn by Jean Shrimpton, Spring–Summer 1971 haute couture collection. Photograph by David Bailey, published in U.S. *Vogue*, March 1971.

paris

SAINT LAURENT:
transparent
chiffon with the
short smoking,
worn by the Tree...
embroidered lace
tunic-pyjamas,
a splurge of
pale flowers,
worn by the Twig

Revealing in the prettiest
way, right: transparent
black chiffon that shows the
perfect jeune-fille bosom—
small, high, rounded—the
shirt for Saint Laurent's new
short smoking. Pants
cropped above the knee,
the jacket—shown closed,
below—as beautifully tail-
ored as a riding habit, in
lightweight black worsted.
Dormeuil fabric. Earrings,
tights, by Saint Laurent. Both
pages: Roger Vivier shoes, to
order at Saks Fifth Avenue.
Blooming tunic-pyjamas, far
right, thickly clustered with
crunchy little bunches of
pink-and-blue flowers
embroidered on lace—
long-sleeved tunic per-
fectly proportioned to the
long narrow pants, both
edged in pink linen....It's
Paris, it's spring, it's abso-
lutely delicious—like a whiff
of Saint Laurent's "Y." Bros-
sin de Méré fabric. I. Mag-
nin. Coiffures by Alexandre.

AVEDON

Breaking away

The first Yves Saint Laurent cut-outs to reveal a glimpse of flesh were stripes across an evening dress designed in 1966. In 1968, the British model Penelope Tree posed for Richard Avedon (ILL. 2) dressed in a tuxedo whose heavily masculine roots are contrasted with a shirt that barely conceals her breasts. A few months later, the Autumn–Winter haute couture collection shown at the rue Spontini included an eye-catching dress that was entirely transparent with – as a gesture to modesty – a single band of black feathers around the hips. In the space of just two years, the 'nude look', as it was called in the American press, became a familiar Yves Saint Laurent motif. Add the scoop-backed dress, veiled in lace rather than chiffon this time, which appeared in the Autumn–Winter 1970–1971 collection and here we see, clearly defined, a pivotal early period in the couturier's creative career. The first half of the 1960s was an opportunity for Christian Dior's successor to bring a repertoire of unusual forms –often based on the fashions of the street – into Paris couture. Leather jackets, trousers and peacoats became declarations of creative emancipation when he launched his first collection in 1962. But by the middle of the decade, the break away from his early designs had become even more pronounced. His first perfume, Y, in 1964, followed by his series of Mondrian dresses, and finally the opening of his store SAINT LAURENT *rive gauche* in 1966, all signalled profound changes. Menswear staples and nautically inspired clothing, the sartorial archetypes that the young designer had reworked in his early days, gave way to a new approach in which the dress was paramount, even when its construction remained innovative. An iconoclastic impulse was turned into a totally new creative process: using a work of art, a source of pictorial inspiration, as the starting point for rethinking a piece of clothing. There is little merit in attempting to uncover the psychological mechanisms at play here, but his two inter-related decisions – to launch, on one hand, his first fragrance and, on the other, his first ready-to-wear collection – are revealing. Having trained as a couturier in the salons of the avenue Montaigne, Yves Saint Laurent was the heir to a tradition that dated back to the previous century. The division of work between the *atelier flou* and the *atelier tailleur*, and the

SEE P. 47

SEE P. 73

SEE P. 78

ILL. 2 Tuxedo suit worn by Penelope Tree, Spring–Summer 1968 haute couture collection. Photograph by Richard Avedon, published in U.S. *Vogue*, March 1968.

fittings for a client who would become the sole and exclusive wearer of a particular garment, set a blueprint for creation and production that Yves Saint Laurent followed diligently when he opened his own couture house. But his move towards a mass-produced and international model of business – as reflected in his perfume line and the ready-to-wear garments of his new label, sold from Paris to London and New York – established a new relationship with the female body. Now more plentiful and often younger than before, his clients helped to redefine the image of the Yves Saint Laurent woman. While his regular in-house models remained recognizable, and his friends and muses could still be seen sporting his designs, Yves Saint Laurent was increasingly – and perhaps paradoxically – dressing a body that was anonymous. Exposing that body, while it may strike us as a way of reducing it to its basic essence, was also an opportunity to give it form and flesh.

Ways of seeing

But what kind of nudity was Yves Saint Laurent really looking to create? The fashion press of the 1950s, which he read assiduously as a teenager, recorded the gradual evolution of beachwear that exposed far more flesh than the demure beach robes of the interwar years ever did. In the U.S. in 1964, Rudi Gernreich outstripped even the most daring sunseekers of the French Riviera with his design for a topless 'monokini', inspired by the concept of a unisex utopia. Legs were bared by British designer Mary Quant, thanks to the miniskirts she sold in her boutique, Bazaar, which opened on London's King's Road in 1955. By the mid-1960s, miniskirts were also a regular sight on the streets of Paris, as Saint Laurent would have observed. But what *he* was looking to create was neither so new, nor so radical.

Rather than fully exposing the body, Yves Saint Laurent was more interested in veiling it. This veiling – or blurring – conveyed a sense of theatricality; the panels of black chiffon and the feathers he ordered from Maison Judith Barbier for his 1968 dress evoked a world of performance that was both familiar and dear to him. In fact, his interest in couture

ILL. 3 Zizi Jeanmaire (wearing Yves Saint Laurent) and Marcel Marceau on the TV programme *Le Show Zizi Jeanmaire*, 13 October 1968. Photograph by Giancarlo Botti.

Casino de Paris
Ballets Roland Petit
Les demoiselles de petite
vertue.

Yves Saint Laurent

ILL. 4 Costume design for the *Les Millionnaires*
tableau from the cabaret show *Zizi Je t'aime!*,
directed by Roland Petit at the Casino de Paris, 1972.

was first displayed, as a very young adult, by designing stage costumes. Later, during his time at Dior, and later running his own couture house, his proximity to the theatres and cabarets of Paris remained a constant. The performer Zizi Jeanmaire, an avid fan of feathered costumes, became a close friend and, over the course of many years, the couturier dressed and undressed her as the whim took him (ILL. 3).

The burlesque nudity of cabaret (ILL. 4) means something very different from nudity on the beach or in the streets. It is built around a new kind of gaze, the gaze of the spectator, whose contemplation of the human body is shaped by the lighting and sets.[3] The spectator's gaze is given focus by the interplay of staging and props, and the quasi-fetishistic segmentation of the dancer's body – into shoulders, legs, belly and breasts – recalls the theories of the historian James Laver, rooted in fantasy and Freudianism, on modesty through the ages.[4] Not everything is visible at one glance; instead, the fascination lies in the way that the gaze shifts from one exposed area to the next. The 'windows' or framed areas that Yves Saint Laurent arranged in order to reveal parts of the body, by means of light through transparent fabric, echo the world of the stage in a very similar way: a world that is chic and scandalous but whose dramatic effects are carefully controlled.

Drawing from life

When Luis Buñuel's film *Belle de Jour* was first screened in May 1967, filmgoers were expecting the director of *L'Âge d'or* to deliver something shocking. The tale of a bored middle-class woman who takes refuge in a fantasy life and begins working in a brothel certainly lived up to their expectations. And by dressing Catherine Deneuve for the role, Yves Saint Laurent was partly responsible for the film's erotic charge. However, the talents of the director and the couturier were driven by a shared belief: the idea that anything that is hidden, veiled or takes place out of sight is far more alluring than a naked body or sex scene captured on camera. In long sleeves and a high neck with a neat collar, Deneuve is demurely dressed by the couturier, with added help from footwear designer Roger Vivier, whose modest-looking buckled pumps are cleverly filmed to become part of the most subversive of erotic fantasies (ILLS. 5 & 6).

3. Antoine de Baecque, 'Écrans. Le corps au cinéma', in Jean-Jacques Courtine (ed.), *Histoire du corps. Tome 3: les mutations du regard, le XXe siècle*, Paris: Seuil, 2005, pp. 371–390.

4. James Laver, *Modesty in Dress: An Inquiry into the Fundamentals of Fashion*, Boston: Houghton Mifflin, 1969.

ILL. 5 Costume design for Catherine Deneuve in the role
of Séverine Serizy in the film *Belle de Jour* (1967), directed
by Luis Buñuel and based on a novel by Joseph Kessel.

ILL. 6 Michel Piccoli, Catherine Deneuve (wearing Yves Saint
Laurent), and Luis Buñuel on the set of *Belle de Jour*, 1966.

ILL. 7 Yves Saint Laurent posing for the ad campaign for *Pour Homme*, his first fragrance for men, Paris, 1971. Photograph by Jeanloup Sieff.

Yves Saint Laurent's contribution to Buñuel's film – which can be viewed, retrospectively, as heralding the arrival of new sexual and social freedoms – raises the question of the 'male gaze', as popularized in film theory by Laura Mulvey.[5] The idea of a male gaze that objectifies women – as a source of inspiration and fantasy – finds particular resonance in the world of haute couture. From the 19th century onwards, a great couturier's reliance on his muse for inspiration reflected precisely this kind of pattern of behaviour. The same rhetoric continued until the 1950s: Christian Dior and Pierre Balmain both projected a particular kind of masculinity in terms of their public image, and embraced an equally normative model of femininity – woman as passive muse or flower.[6] Yves Saint Laurent disrupted this legacy in more ways than one. Like the women of his generation who were about to be swept along by a new wave of feminism, his discreet affirmation of his own identity as a gay man (despite ongoing legal constraints) placed him in a position where he was fighting to establish his own identity and achieve social recognition. Just as he explored the idea of 'unveiling' the female body in his collections, he did much the same thing with his own body when he chose to appear naked in front of Jeanloup Sieff's camera for a perfume advertisement in 1971 (ILL. 7). Nudity, albeit partial, as revealed by the couturier's sheer designs, was a bid to throw off the shackles of bourgeois convention, just as Saint Laurent himself was doing, both as a fashion designer and as a man in his own right.

But what is it saying, this male – and queer, in contemporary terminology – gaze, which appears to liberate the nude from its purely erotic or seductive qualities? It is nudity that is carefully concealed and veiled, not merely revealed by manipulating necklines and hemlines in the most straightforward manner. It is here that the connection with art history provides some insight: while Yves Saint Laurent's work is fond of the Pop Art game of appropriation and quotation, here a more classical connection can be made. In traditional art, the word *académie* referred to the exercise of drawing from life, and from the 19th century onwards – in the work of Ingres for example (ILL. 8) – the nude model was often female. The *académie* marked an important step in an artist's education, implying a level of technical mastery and aesthetic accomplishment. The bare female breasts that began to feature in Yves Saint Laurent's collections in

5. Laura Mulvey, 'Visual Pleasure and Narrative Cinema' (1973), *Visual and Other Pleasures,* London: Palgrave Macmillan, 1989.

6. Christopher Breward, 'Couture as Queer Auto/ Biography', in Valerie Steele (ed.), *A Queer History of Fashion: From the Closet to the Catwalk,* New Haven: Yale University Press, 2013.

the mid-1960s might be described as a sartorial equivalent of this drawing from life. Neither indecent nor ignored, they can be viewed as a classical motif, a timeless academic exercise. This idea is elegantly affirmed by the gilded metal bodyplates created by Claude Lalanne, cast from the models' own bodies, that featured in Yves Saint Laurent's Autumn–Winter 1969–1970 haute couture collection (ILL. 9, ILL. 10).

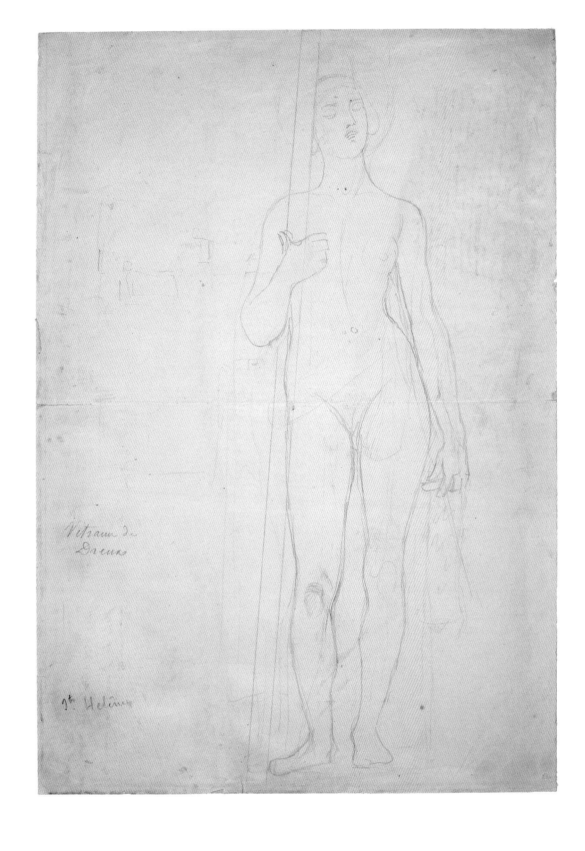

Vitraux de
Dreux

St Hélène

ILL. 8 Jean-Auguste-Dominique Ingres, Nude study for the figure of *St Helena*, for the stained glass windows of the Chapelle Saint Ferdinand des Ternes, 1842, pencil on paper, 38.7 × 27 cm. Bayonne, Musée Bonnat-Helleu.

Esther sur Lisa 1070

ILL. 9 Original sketch for an evening gown,
Autumn–Winter 1969–1970 haute couture collection.

ILL. 10 Evening gown worn by Lisa,
with sculpted metal element by Claude Lalanne,
Autumn–Winter 1969–1970 haute couture collection.
Salons at 30*bis* rue Spontini, Paris, 27 July 1969.

Yves Saint Laurent: Unveiling, displaying, adorning

Shazia Boucher

The body and transparency

From the moment he founded his couture house in 1961, Yves Saint Laurent's efforts were focused on unveiling women's bodies to the world. He created designs that played with the idea of transparency through cutting, draping and layering. He introduced openings in garments that were like windows onto the body, revealing, in turn, breasts, back, waist, belly, hips, buttocks, legs and arms. He clothed the body in light, sheer fabrics – lace, tulle, chiffon, Cigaline® and organza. And he used sequins, ribbons, feathers and other embellishments to create transparent effects that were less obvious, more mysterious. Throughout his career, he pursued the same goal, shaping a female figure that could be recognized by her slender outline, her meticulous makeup and her clothes that were inspired by the traditional male wardrobe yet retained a sensuality that was altogether feminine.

The body unveiled

'A woman's naked body, which I must dress without impeding the freedom of her natural movements. In short, my metier is the tender dialogue between that naked woman and all the magical folds of my fabrics.'[1] — Yves Saint Laurent

The first collections Yves Saint Laurent designed after opening his couture house remained faithful to the aesthetic canons of haute couture and did nothing to upset contemporary notions of propriety. Nevertheless, he was already starting to play with the idea of transparency and layered fabric effects. There were plunging necklines and exposed upper backs; arms were bare or clearly visible beneath sheer fabrics. But it was not until 1966 that Yves Saint Laurent offered up his first genuinely revealing outfits – a set of short dresses in sheer organza, embroidered with sequins that formed stripes or chevrons strategically positioned around the breasts and hips, leaving the upper chest, belly and tops of the legs exposed (ILL. 2, ILL. 3).

1. Handwritten note, Musée Yves Saint Laurent Paris archives.

ILL. 1 Evening ensemble worn by Mounia Orosemane, Spring–Summer 1978 haute couture collection. Hôtel InterContinental, Paris, 25 January 1978. Photograph by Claus Ohm.

45

4139
Simone
Ana

Ana

Transparent magic—
the barely there dresses.
Beautifully flimsy idea
by Yves Saint Laurent.
A layer of organza
and a handful of sequins.
Organza by Bianchini.
Hair by Edward of
André Bernard.
Lipstick, Payot's Pastel

The blouse was always a key piece in the couturier's stylistic repertoire, and appeared in his collections from the very start. The sheer version worn with a tuxedo jacket and Bermuda shorts that forms part of the Spring–Summer 1968 collection[2] is slightly loose-fitting and very feminine; it's made from a type of Cigaline® that reveals the nude torso beneath, and accessorized with a pussycat bow in black silk satin. Remaining true to his motto that 'fashions change, but style is eternal', Yves Saint Laurent would continue to produce blouses in multiples variations right up until his final haute couture collection of 2002.

SEE P. 70

The body displayed

'Nothing is more beautiful than a naked body. The most beautiful clothes that can dress a woman are the arms of the man she loves. But for those who have not been lucky enough to find that happiness, I am there.'[3]
— Yves Saint Laurent

From 1966 onwards, Yves Saint Laurent invented many ways of revealing a woman's body. Dresses with cut-out panels, creating a range of geometric effects, drew attention to different areas of the body. A series of short dresses from Spring–Summer 1966 perfectly illustrate this principle, the black silk crepe fabric contrasting with the bare skin of the wearer's back, belly and waist (ILL. 4). An evening gown in the Autumn–Winter 1990–1991 collection pushes the approach to its extreme: a long panel of black sequinned lace is wrapped around the wearer's body and simply held in place by two large bows of pink silk satin, leaving the side of the body bare (ILL. 7).

SEE P. 68

Sometimes these windows onto the body are veiled with lace, which heightens rather than hides the sensuality of the bare skin beneath. Yves Saint Laurent was aware of his role as a pioneer in this regard: 'I was the first to reveal a woman's breasts, but now they advance down the catwalk naked....'[4] The couturier was a trailblazer, playfully exploring the ambiguities of underwear-as-outerwear long before this trend caught on more widely

2. All the outfits mentioned in this article are part of the haute couture collections.

3. Handwritten note, Musée Yves Saint Laurent Paris archives.

4. Yves Saint Laurent quoted in Laurence Benaim, *Yves Saint Laurent*, Paris, Grasset, 2018, p. 620.

ILL. 4 Dresses worn by Beate Schulz Moore, Sunny Griffin and Agneta Darin, Spring–Summer 1966 haute couture collection. Photograph by James Moore, published in *Harper's Bazaar*, March 1966.

ILL. 5 Dress worn by Georgianna Robertson, Spring–Summer 1999
haute couture collection. Hôtel InterContinental, Paris, 20 January 1999.

ILL. 6 Ensemble worn by Naomi Campbell, Spring–Summer 1999 haute
couture collection. Hôtel InterContinental, Paris, 20 January 1999.

in the 1990s. One example is his Autumn–Winter 1990–1991 collection with its 'boudoir dresses' in gossamer-fine lace, and lingerie-inspired details such as satin ribbons, frills and boning. He also made a feature of bras: worn beneath a trouser suit for Spring–Summer 1978; under a shirt in transparent Cigaline® for Spring–Summer 1999 (ILL. 6); and teamed with a skirt of fringed lace for Spring–Summer 2000.

The body adorned

> 'With women, it's not just about austerity and precise lines.
> There needs to be an element of dreaming, of sensuality.
> What could be more beautiful than to portray them as
> birds of paradise?'[5]
> — Yves Saint Laurent

In his quest to create gorgeous evening attire for women, Yves Saint Laurent made lace work to his advantage, using it to showcase different parts of the body, and light, sheer fabrics – such as chiffon, crepe georgette and lace – often featured in his most ornate designs. The lace tended to be black Chantilly lace, although heavier laces in a guipure style were also well represented.

Lace itself can also be transformed in various ways, even to the point of becoming unrecognizable. This final stage, known as *ennoblissement* or finishing, might take place at the lace manufacturers, in specialist ateliers, or at the couture house itself. Designs for evening wear offered an ideal opportunity to combine different materials – lace and rhinestone cabochons, for example, in a short evening dress from the Spring–Summer 1980 collection. A sheath dress designed for Autumn–Winter 1984–1985 has a wonderful shimmer thanks to sequins embroidered over the lace. It forms part of a collection that uses sequinned lace manufactured (for the most part) by Maison Marescot, and intended primarily for evening wear.

Another exquisitely delicate combination is a short lace bustier dress with a broad sash belt, worn with a coat made from bird-of-paradise feathers. Lace can also serve as a backing for an all-over embroidery that

SEE P. 76

5. *Ibid.*, p. 527.

ILL. 7 Original sketch for an evening gown, Autumn–Winter 1990–1991 haute couture collection.

ILL. 8, P. 54 Evening gown worn by Rebecca Ayoko, Autumn–Winter 1985–1986 haute couture collection. Hôtel InterContinental, Paris, 24 July 1985. Photograph by Guy Marineau.

ILL. 9, P. 55 Gown worn by Noémie Lenoir, Spring–Summer 2000 haute couture collection. Hôtel InterContinental, Paris, 19 January 2000.

almost conceals the fabric beneath, as in the case of the sheath dress for Autumn–Winter 1996–1997 made from Marescot lace entirely embroidered with pink chenille yarn, black and silver 'garland' yarn and pink sequins. Also worthy of mention is the unusual combination of floral print and black lace for a dress in the Spring–Summer 2000 collection (ILL. 9). The printed skirt fabric is edged with a panel of lace and the lace bodice is decorated with sequinned embroidery that echoes the flower motif of the fabric.

     In collection after collection throughout his career, Yves Saint Laurent adopted different approaches to transparency as a means of showing off a woman's body, utilizing a rich decorative palette of lace and embroidery. Over the years, an iconic feminine look emerged, denoting a woman who was both powerful and sensual.

Wearing the sheer look: Rebecca Ayoko remembers

Domitille Éblé

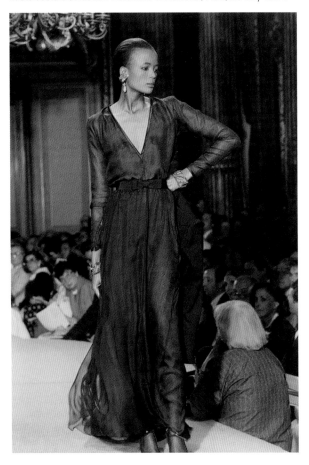

Evening gown worn by Rebecca Ayoko, Autumn–Winter 1984–1985 haute couture collection. Hôtel InterContinental, Paris, 25 July 1984.

In addition to being a raw material and a technique, sheerness can also be a lived experience. The wearer learns what sheerness means – what it means to expose her body to the couturier's gaze during a fitting, to the gaze of the audience on the runway, and to guests and the media at a social event.

In order to understand what that experience was like, we wanted to talk to a former Yves Saint Laurent model, Rebecca Ayoko, about her memories of wearing the sheer look.[1]

Rebecca Ayoko joined the Maison in June 1983 and continued to model its haute couture collections until Autumn–Winter 1987–1988. She was one of the 'studio models'[2] who were involved at every stage of a new collection, from preparation to the final show. These young women waited in what was known as the 'cabine' for a summons from the couturier's studio, if they were required to help with the design process; they later modelled the toiles and, finally, the finished garments at the various fittings. If Yves Saint Laurent did not already have an idea for his collection in mind,[3] he would begin by observing the bodies of his models and then making sketches.

Models wore a simple uniform comprising panties, black tights, black pumps and a white robe. When they went up to the studio, the robe would come off and they would pose in front of the full-length mirror. The aim was to spark the couturier's creative impulses. 'By the time I was standing in front of him, I was undressed, there were no more taboos,' Rebecca Ayoko explains, recalling this rather unusual ritual. Yves Saint Laurent might make a sketch there and then, in front of his unclothed model. Afterwards, he would call the ateliers to explain his design and what he wished to see translated into three dimensions, first in the form of the toile and later using the chosen fabrics for the collection. Sometimes he would drape a piece of fabric around the model. 'It was at that point that the garment came alive', Rebecca Ayoko says. He would study the way the fabric moved and reacted on the body by observing it in the mirror, but rarely looked directly at the model herself, preferring to judge her reflection instead.

Rebecca Ayoko remembers that very little was said in the studio: it was all about looking. Yves Saint Laurent would put the models at their ease with a few words or simply by making eye contact. There was a sense of harmony that the couturier described in the following way: 'When I design and craft my dresses, I need a living model, a moving body. I could never work with a mere wooden mannequin because for me clothes must live. I need to work with a woman's body before sending out my clothes into the real world.'[4]

In Rebecca Ayoko's opinion, transparency was never vulgar in Yves Saint Laurent's work. He created a look that was elegant and chic, and the idea of being deliberately provocative was far from his mind. She compares the art of *deshabillé* with the art of shadow play: we see a shape and that shape suggests a silhouette, a body. Yves Saint Laurent's aim was to suggest nudity rather than to expose the body completely: 'Transparency is something with which I have long been familiar. The important thing with transparency is to retain the mystery,'[5] he himself declared. Delicate, flowing fabrics simply gave an impression of the nudity that lay beneath. And in modelling these creations for the public, Ayoko claims that she did not feel naked – despite wearing garments that were in fact transparent – but, rather, as if her body were being validated.

Evening ensemble worn by Rebecca Ayoko, Autumn–Winter 1984–1985 haute couture collection. Polaroid taken by a staff member.

According to Rebecca Ayoko, there was nothing especially difficult about wearing transparent clothing on the catwalk. Perhaps the context alters the way a woman's body is viewed. Think, for example, of French actor and model Laetitia Casta, who wore a 'nude dress' to the César Awards in 2010. While her arrival attracted a great deal of attention and the press focused on her sheer outfit as being the most noteworthy element of the evening, Casta herself – a veteran of the catwalk – seems to have taken the whole experience in her stride.

1. Rebecca Ayoko was interviewed on 7 November 2022 by Shazia Boucher and Domitille Éblé.

2. Like the cabine models (who worked in-house full time), they modelled clothes for clients wanting to purchase an outfit and were present at the fittings. Studio models might also take part in the runway shows. Some models were only involved in the latter.

3. Yves Saint Laurent usually designed his collections in Marrakesh, twice a year, in December and June.

4. Handwritten note conserved at the Musée Yves Saint Laurent Paris.

5. From an interview with Laurence Benaïm on 12 January 2002 and included in Benaïm's biography *Yves Saint Laurent*, Paris: Grasset, 2018, pp. 679–680.

Sketching the sheer

Domitille Éblé

Colette

7371

mousseline
rose

Sketching occupied a primordial place in Yves Saint Laurent's work. It was the foundation for all his creations and the way in which he expressed his thoughts. It served as proof of his original idea, it embodied the very essence of his style, and it never lied. Sometimes, to reveal the lines of a body or to indicate transparency, he would need to draw a woman's breasts or buttocks. By examining three looks that typify his approach to transparency, we will look at the way the couturier represented sheer fabric on paper.

In Spring–Summer 1968, Yves Saint Laurent introduced his first transparent blouse, teamed with a tuxedo jacket. In the original sketch for this look (ILL. 2), the blouse is only partly visible: the couturier has chosen to sketch the outfit with the jacket buttoned up, as if the transparent element was not yet a given and he was waiting to see how it would be received in the ateliers and, later, on the catwalk. It was a different story when it came to depicting the same outfit in an illustration (ILL. 3) for the Yves Saint Laurent exhibition at New York's Metropolitan Museum fifteen years later, in 1983.[1] Almost certainly inspired by the pose adopted by Danielle Luquet de Saint Germain that was captured by photographer Peter Caine in 1968,[2] Yves Saint Laurent depicts his model standing with her hands thrust into the pockets of her Bermuda shorts and her breasts visible. In contrast with the earlier sketch, this one suggests total confidence: the outfit had caused a commotion when it was first shown, but that had now passed and transparency had become an integral ingredient of the Yves Saint Laurent style.

The following season – Autumn–Winter 1968–1969 – Yves Saint Laurent showed his 'nude dress'. This time, the transparency of the chiffon is represented in the original sketch by light hatching (ILL. 4), with details of the wearer's breasts and belt drawn underneath, indicating, for the benefit of the ateliers, dressers and models, how the dress should be worn – with the breasts showing through the fabric and a belt worn beneath the dress, next to the skin. The figure is depicted mid-stride to show off the fullness of the shape, which is given structure by the band of feathers around the hips. In all the documents recording the creation of this dress,[3] the model is always shown in motion, both to indicate how the garment is structured (cut on the bias), and to evoke the image of an active, modern, liberated

1. *Yves Saint Laurent, 25 Years of Design*, New York: Metropolitan Museum of Art, 14 December 1983– 2 September 1984.

2. See 'Sheer provocation', p. 70, below.

3. The original sketch, the research sketch, the atelier specification sheet (or 'Bible page'), and the collection board.

ILL. 1 Original sketch of a blouse and pair of trousers for a tuxedo, Spring–Summer 1999 haute couture collection.

ILL. 2, P. 62 Original sketch for a tuxedo, Spring–Summer 1968 haute couture collection.

ILL. 3, P. 63 Sketch of the 1968 tuxedo made by Yves Saint Laurent in 1983 for the catalogue of the exhibition *Yves Saint Laurent: 25 Years of Design*, Metropolitan Museum of Art, New York.

3058

1 50A
B 35A

Mielle

Yves Saint
CROQUIS N°

woman. Following the success of the transparent blouse, sheerness was now accepted as a given from the first sketch.

The same is true of the iconic scoop-back dress in Chantilly lace created for the Autumn–Winter 1970–1971 collection. The lace, as is usually the case in Yves Saint Laurent's sketches, is indicated with undulating lines. In the original sketch (ILL. 5), the couturier emphasizes the cleft between the buttocks to demonstrate just how low the back should be cut: the ateliers would have been in no doubt as to the deliberately daring nature of the look. In the 1983 illustration (ILL. 7), the cleft is simply an extension of the spinal column and the model's pose recalls that of Marina Schiano in the photograph taken by Jeanloup Sieff.[4]

Yves Saint Laurent's sketches enable us to observe the evolution of transparency in the couturier's work and its inclusion at the earliest stage in the creative process. Lace was represented by curvy lines, sheer fabrics such as chiffon, Cigaline® and organza chiefly by hatching, and covered areas of the female body were depicted in order to show just how that body would look beneath the sheer fabric (ILL. 1).

4. See 'Sheer vertigo', p. 77, below.

ILL. 4 Original sketch for an evening gown, Autumn–Winter 1968–1969 haute couture collection.

4109
Esther
Danielle
mousseline
noire.

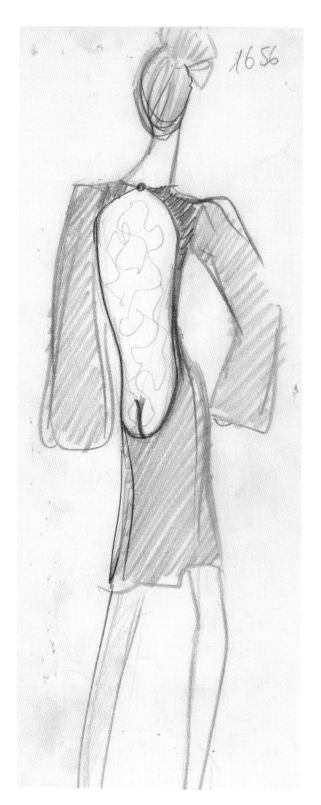

ILLS. 5 & 6   Original sketches for an evening dress (back and front), Autumn–Winter 1970–1971 haute couture collection.

ILL. 7   Sketch of the 1970–1971 dress made by Yves Saint Laurent in 1983 for the catalogue of the exhibition *Yves Saint Laurent: 25 Years of Design*, Metropolitan Museum of Art, New York.

Sheer provocation

Judith Lamas

An air of youth and imagination wafted through the creations of Yves Saint Laurent's Spring–Summer 1968 haute couture collection. It was a wardrobe for women clearly inspired by tailoring for men. Trousers, jumpsuits and Bermuda shorts were the leading looks.

With this sense of whimsy, the couturier reinvented some of his classic pieces, often for evening wear, with the most striking example being the tuxedo – *le smoking*. His brand new version, shorter and more daring – comprised a long jacket and Bermuda shorts in grain de poudre (manufactured by Dormeuil), teamed with a diaphanous blouse in Cigaline® (by Bucol), finished at the neck with a pussycat bow in silk satin (ILL. 1).

This evening ensemble was a bold bid to free feminine charms. By exposing the breasts, the Cigaline® serves to showcase the wearer's most feminine assets, while the Bermuda shorts reveal her legs. This fusion of transparency and nudity is seductive and sensual but avoids vulgarity. The model, Danielle Luquet de Saint Germain, wore the outfit with such panache that it seemed almost natural to see her dressed in this way. There were many strong reactions, however, from the press and the world of haute couture. This kind of transgression of fashion norms was bound to provoke a lively discussion in newspapers as to whether the outfit, though 'charming', could truly be worn in everyday life or whether it should be deemed too provocative.

Yves Saint Laurent enjoyed being provocative. Although naturally shy, he confidently declared that he had had enough of 'daisy-covered breasts'[1] and that 'it was important to have a bit of fun'.[2] 'I mean it as a serious fashion. I'll probably show more bare dresses for the autumn. This is a fashion which must come.'[3]

'Fluidity' was the key word of the Autumn–Winter 1968–1969 haute couture collection. The 'nude look' may seem like an odd choice for a winter collection; nonetheless, some of those looks became Yves Saint Laurent landmarks. Among them was a 'full-length chiffon evening gown'[4] in black silk (from Bianchini-Férier), which was entirely transparent and adorned, at hip level, with a band of tone-on-tone ostrich feathers (by the feather artist Judith Barbier) that skilfully concealed the most intimate parts of the wearer's body (ILL. 2). Despite its apparent simplicity, this creation – made in-house, in Madame Esther's *atelier flou* – was technically audacious in

1. Yves Saint Laurent, in 'Sex hits Paris for six', *Daily Mirror*, 24 February 1968.

2. Yves Saint Laurent, in 'La Mode. Il ne faut pas enlever la veste', *France-Soir – Paris-Presse, L'Intransigeant*, 26 February 1968.

3. Yves Saint Laurent, in 'Eves, St. Laurent', *The Sun*, 30 January 1968.

4. As described in the programme for the collection.

ILL. 1 Tuxedo worn by Danielle Luquet de Saint Germain, Spring–Summer 1968 haute couture collection. Photograph by Peter Caine.

its construction. Far from damaging the very delicate chiffon, the feather belt was an integral part of the garment and helped to give it structure. Completing the look was a narrow decorative belt in gilded bronze, with a double snake's-head fastening, designed to be worn next to the skin, and a pair of low-heeled gold leather pumps.

This diaphanous, gorgeously sensuous gown was modelled at that season's show by Danielle Luquet de Saint Germain. The way the dress was cut – its flow and fluidity – was strikingly dynamic. The chiffon showed off the model's body, her breasts, her every curve, all her feminine attributes. Like a contemporary Eve, she looked naked, but with a nakedness that seemed almost primal. This kind of nudity was more than a mere manifesto of transparency: it echoed the sexual revolution ushered in by the 1960s. Yves Saint Laurent was well attuned to these contemporary issues. Seductiveness and freedom from convention would become creative leitmotifs that characterized his whole career.

Yves Saint Laurent succeeded in breaking the rules of fashion and of haute couture. He was resolutely daring in his bid to reveal what, in his view, was the essence of femininity, firmly believing that 'Nothing is more beautiful than a naked body.'[5]

5. Handwritten note by Yves Saint Laurent, Musée Yves Saint Laurent Paris archives.

ILL. 2 Evening gown worn by Danielle Luquet de Saint
Germain, Autumn–Winter 1968–1969 haute couture
collection. Contact sheet of photographs by Peter Caine.

ILL. 3 Evening gown worn by Magali Lemoine, Autumn–Winter 1993–1994 haute couture collection. Hôtel InterContinental, Paris, 21 July 1993. Photograph by Guy Marineau.

ILL. 4 Ensemble worn by Naomi Campbell, Autumn–Winter 1988–1989 SAINT LAURENT *rive gauche* collection. Cour Carrée, the Louvre, Paris, 23 March 1988. Photograph by Guy Marineau.

Sheer vertigo

Alice Coulon-Saillard

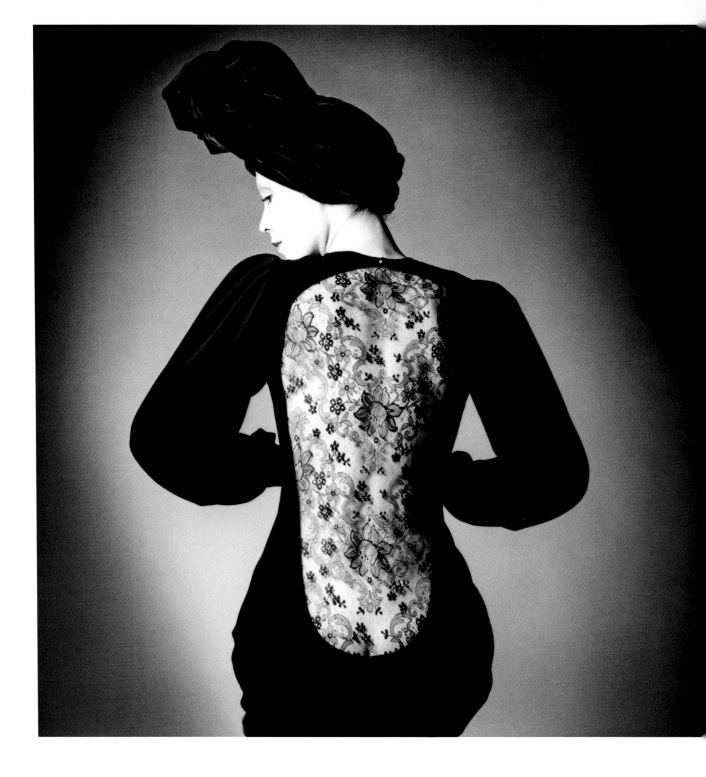

At first glance, the famous evening gown from Yves Saint Laurent's Autumn–Winter 1970–1971 haute couture collection looks very restrained – deeply black, with long, flowing sleeves and a row of black buttons reaching up to a high neckline. It is at the *back* of the dress where all its playfulness and sensuality lie.

Yves Saint Laurent created a great many backless designs. Here, he took backlessness to another level by deepening the scoop of the back down to the top of the buttocks and veiling the bared skin in lace. The effect is dizzying, the wearer's skin showing through the lace like a subtle and seductive conjuring trick, a case of 'now you see me, now you don't'. By slightly distancing the viewer, the sheer fabric enhances the boldness of the design, making the contrast with the front of the garment even more striking.

This knee-length dress, immortalized by photographer Jeanloup Sieff (1933–2000), appeared in *Vogue* Paris in September 1970. Bathed in light, the bare back of model Marina Schiano (1941–2019) is revealed from her shoulders to the top of her buttocks, beneath the screen of Chantilly lace (ILL. 1). The delicacy of this portrait is the result of the photographer's supreme mastery of the art of shooting in black and white. Jeanloup Sieff worked for many top fashion magazines in the 1970s and was instrumental in helping to advertise the Maison Yves Saint Laurent.

'I am not a fashion photographer, but sometimes in my work, pleasure has come from clothes. And these rare photographic pleasures have always been thanks to Yves Saint Laurent,'[1] Sieff said in 1997. In this rear-view portrait, the model's pose, her partial nudity and the turban on her head all echo a famous image by Man Ray (1890–1976), *Le Violon d'Ingres* (1924), which shows a naked Kiki de Montparnasse (1901–1953) with her back to the camera, creating a silhouette that emulates the curves of a cello. Yves Saint Laurent almost certainly had that famous photograph in mind when he designed his Autumn–Winter 1979–1980 haute couture collection. One of the looks from that show – which was a homage to Serge de Diaghilev (1872–1929), director of the Ballets Russes, and to his collaboration with Pablo Picasso (1881–1973) – was a 'guitar dress in velvet and embroidered black lace'[2] (ILL. 2).

In his research sketches for that gown, the couturier added the cello's sound holes on the lace-covered back (ILL. 3). These two stylized

1. Béatrice Dupire and Hady Sy (eds.), *Yves Saint Laurent: Forty Years of Creation*, New York, International Festival of Fashion Photography, 1998.

2. Programme for the Autumn–Winter 1979–1980 haute couture collection.

ILL. 1 Marina Schiano wearing an evening dress, Autumn–Winter 1970–1971 haute couture collection. Photograph by Jeanloup Sieff, published in *Vogue* Paris, September 1970.

At Saint Laurent...

Big-Evening Dressing With the Most Bareness!

The surprise: velvet and lace used for maximum revealing. Yves' last-word in P.M. dare! *Above:* The longest cling of black velvet (Leonard) inset with a sinuous curve of lace—if you're of the school that thinks velvet-and-lace is old-fashioned, look again! What you don't see: the front— "diamond" and jet buttons, a center slit, and the kicker—a small flirty train! Yves Saint Laurent Accessories. Exclusively at Holt Renfrew of Canada, to order only.

FRANCOIS LAMY

arabesque motifs are not present on the finished dress, but they highlight the connection with Man Ray's photograph, on which the sound holes are drawn in Indian ink. The gown of 1979–1980 was a full-length version of the 1970–1971 knee-length dress, now embellished with alternating black and rhinestone buttons, and with a slightly more open neckline and a split at the hem to allow greater freedom of movement. The model wearing this revealing dress was deliberately styled with her hair loose and struck a more openly seductive pose. This intention was picked up by the contemporary press, which reported that the models in the show seemed totally confident, verging on provocative.

The influence of the fashion of the 1940s, as reflected in the 1970–1971 evening dress,[3] was also visible in the Spring–Summer 1996 haute couture collection (ILL. 4, ILL. 5). A dress in wool crepe and lace offered a playful mix of restraint and sensuality. Its deep scoop back was veiled with lace embroidered with black sequins, forming stylized flower motifs and highlighting the transparency of the fabric by drawing attention to the wearer's skin. The cut-out motif was more heavily accentuated than in the earlier versions, now forming a heart shape above the waist and revealing the wearer's bottom below. Like a declaration of love for womankind, the erotic audacity that Yves Saint Laurent had embraced early in his career was taken to another level in this late work, cheekily exaggerated and helping to liberate the female body.

3. For his next haute couture collection, Spring–Summer 1971, Yves Saint Laurent once again took his inspiration from 1940s fashion. This so-called 'Liberation' collection caused a great deal of press controversy.

ILL. 2, PP. 80–81 Evening dress, Autumn–Winter 1979–1980 haute couture collection. Photograph by François Lamy, published in *Harper's Bazaar*, October 1979.

ILL. 3 Original sketch for an evening gown, Autumn–Winter 1979–1980 haute couture collection.

55 RUE DE BABYL

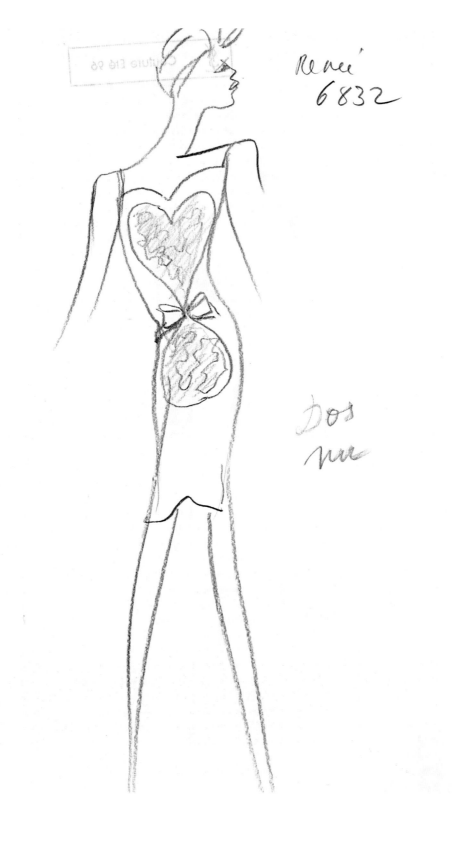

Renee
6832

Couture Eté 96

Dos
nu

ILL. 4 Original sketch for an evening dress,
Spring–Summer 1996 haute couture collection.

ILL. 5 Dress worn by Karen Mulder, Spring–Summer
1996 haute couture collection. Hôtel InterContinental, Paris,
24 January 1996. Photograph by Claus Ohm.

Yves Saint Laurent and lace

Sophie Henwood

in collaboration with Domitille Éblé

Bolero (detail), 2000 Spring–Summer haute couture collection. Photograph by Patricia Canino.

'With a dress, the most important thing is the material, in other words fabric and colour. You can make a fancy design. You can channel all your professional know-how into a design. But if you don't have the material, your dress is a lost cause […]'

In an interview with Yvonne Baby for *Le Monde* in 1983, Yves Saint Laurent listed his favourite textiles: 'Linen, velvet (especially), satin, men's fabrics (Prince of Wales check, pinstripes, tweed), waterproof silks, tulle, Ottoman, any military-style fabric (woollen cloth, unbleached cotton, tarpaulin, naval white cotton) and peacoat flannel.'

Yves Saint Laurent is not a name that is automatically associated with lace. In fact, many of his most iconic designs, often inspired by men's wardrobe staples such as the trench coat and the tuxedo, seem poorly suited to the use of such an intrinsically feminine fabric.

While not a dominant feature, this striking fabric is nevertheless very much present in the couturier's collections. Of the 8,250 haute couture designs he created between 1962 and 2002, some 3,100 are conserved at the Musée Yves Saint Laurent Paris. Among these, including the garments conserved at the Cité de la Dentelle et de la Mode, some three hundred designs[1] are wholly or partially made of lace: in other words, around ten per cent. Using this museum material and its documentation, it is our aim to discuss the characteristics, provenance and usage of lace within the couturier's creative output.

Lace: technique and history

The lace in question is machine-made. Multiple threads are woven together to create the ground and the motifs simultaneously, using a Leavers loom (named after its inventor). The resulting textile is hard-wearing and offers almost limitless creative potential. While it was developed in the 1830s as an imitation of handmade lace, over the course of the 20th century, machine lace came to be seen as a luxury product, the fruit of unique craftsmanship and technical skill. In France it was mainly produced in Calais, Caudry and the area around Lyon[2] (ILL. 1, ILL. 2).

1. Source: Musée Yves Saint Laurent Paris collections management database; search term: 'lace' (November 2022).

2. Only Calais (Pas-de-Calais) and Caudry (Nord) continue to manufacture lace today.

ILL. 1 Leavers lace machine manufactured by Quillet, Calais, 20th century, presented to the Cité de la Dentelle et de la Mode.

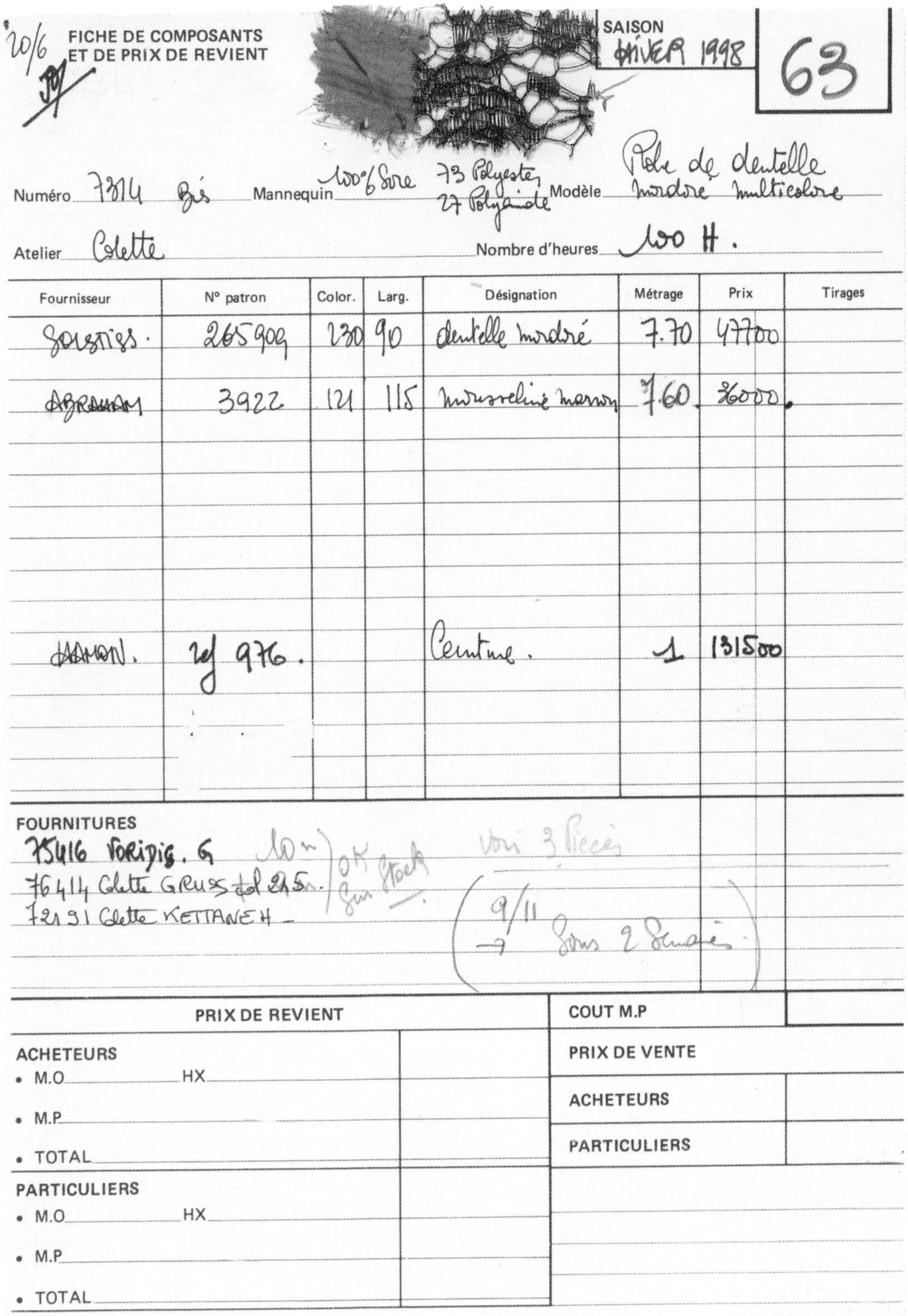

FICHE DE COMPOSANTS
ET DE PRIX DE REVIENT

SAISON
HIVER 1998

63

Numéro 7314 Bis   Mannequin _100% Soie 73 Polyester 27 Polyamide_   Modèle _Robe de dentelle mordoré multicolore_

Atelier Colette   Nombre d'heures _100 H._

Fournisseur	N° patron	Color.	Larg.	Désignation	Métrage	Prix	Tirages
Solstiss.	265909	230	90	dentelle mordré	7.70	47700	
Abraham	3922	121	115	mousseline marron	7.60	26000.	
Hamon.	2y 976.			Ceinture.	1	131500	

FOURNITURES
75416 Toridis. G   10m   OK sur stock   voir 3 Pièces
76414 Colette GRUSS 215.
72191 Colette KETTANEH _   9/11
                                → Sous 2 Semaines.

PRIX DE REVIENT		COUT M.P	
ACHETEURS		**PRIX DE VENTE**	
• M.O HX			
• M.P		**ACHETEURS**	
• TOTAL		**PARTICULIERS**	
PARTICULIERS			
• M.O HX			
• M.P			
• TOTAL			

ILL. 2 Evening gown in Solstiss iridescent lace (detail),
Autumn–Winter 1998–1999 haute couture collection.
Photograph by Patricia Canino.

ILL. 3 Handling record for a dress in Solstiss lace,
Autumn–Winter 1998–1999 haute couture collection.

When Yves Saint Laurent and Pierre Bergé opened their couture house in 1961, Leavers lace was at a crossroads in its history. The previous decade had seen the birth of a new type of machine lace, which was knitted rather than woven. Marketed under the name 'Raschel', it was much faster and cheaper to produce, but inferior in quality. To counter the competition, the Chambre Syndicale des Dentelles et Broderies established the 'Dentelle de Calais'[3] label in 1958. Nevertheless, this threat, along with the younger generation's waning interest in lace and the advent of ready-to-wear, which introduced broader access to more cheaply produced fashions, created havoc in the lacemaking industry. From the 1960s up until the early 21st century, haute couture and luxury ready-to-wear became key outlets for manufacturers of high-quality textiles. By purchasing from these manufacturers, the Maison Yves Saint Laurent helped to sustain the businesses that designed and manufactured Leavers lace and so safeguard the industry's technical excellence and skill.

Lacemakers of Calais, Caudry and Lyon

Like other leading couture houses, the Maison Yves Saint Laurent sourced its fabrics from the most renowned manufacturers. Its archives, which are housed at its Paris museum, are a rich source of information on those suppliers. The handling records[4] (ILL. 3) list all the elements required to create a particular garment: description, reference number, colour-way, quantity, price and supplier. A close analysis of these documents, therefore, allows us to draw up a reasonably comprehensive list of lace manufacturers. The current study is based on a sample[5] of what the Maison produced, and features the following names: Dognin, Brivet, Hurel, Marescot, Solstiss and Darquer. The list is certainly not exhaustive and, while all the names that appear here are French, not all appear with the same regularity.

      One of the lesser-known firms (recorded around a dozen times at most) is Dognin, one of the earliest firms to manufacture tulle and later lace. Founded in Lyon in 1805, and with factories in Villeurbanne and Calais, Dognin is recorded on the handling records of ten designs between

3. The label referred exclusively to lace produced on Leavers machines in France. It was renamed Dentelle de Calais-Caudry® in 2012.

4. The Musée Yves Saint Laurent Paris holds handling records for all haute couture designs between 1967 and 2002.

5. The lace garments conserved in the museum collections (Paris and Calais).

ILL. 4 Evening gown in Dognin lace (detail), Autumn–Winter 1966–1967 haute couture collection. Cité de la Dentelle et de la Mode collection, Calais. Photograph by Patricia Canino.

1962 and 1966 (ILL. 4). The company was badly affected when the fashion industry began to fall out of love with lace in the mid-1960s and went out of business in 1985. Darquer, by contrast, is still operating today.[6] Founded in Calais in 1840, it is one of the oldest firms in the city. The brand Solstiss, formed by a merger of five older Caudry lacemaking firms[7] in 1974, only appears in the records occasionally.

The Maison Yves Saint Laurent seems to have done most of its business with the manufacturers Hurel and Marescot. Hurel originally specialized in embroidery, but eventually broadened its scope to include all luxury textiles. After acquiring the Calais-based firm of Brivet in 1971, it began supplying lace to couture houses. The records include several dozen references to Hurel between 1973 and 1996. Brivet had formerly been a supplier to the Maison Yves Saint Laurent since the 1960s: notably, their lace was used for the evening coat in 'smoky grey' Chantilly now in the collection of the Calais museum [8] (ILL. 5). By far the most popular supplier, however, was Riechers-Marescot, another historic collaborator of Yves Saint Laurent, in operation in Calais since the 1880s. Even when it was bought up by Sophie Hallette, another Leavers lace manufacturer, in 1997, the firm continued to be listed on the handling records under its old name. Marescot lace featured in almost all of Yves Saint Laurent's collections, and in eighteen out of the 182 creations shown in the Autumn–Winter 1984–1985 collection (ILL. 7). The same manufacturer also contributed sequinned lace (ILL. 8) and raffia-embroidered lace.[9]

Yves Saint Laurent designed his garments first and then selected the fabrics. While his fashion house made use of exclusive products from several craft disciplines (embroidery, printed textiles, feather work, jewelry), when it came to lace, it seems that he always used existing designs, pre-selected at the manufacturers' sales offices by his colleagues. No evidence has been found to suggest that he ever had lace specially commissioned for any of his collections.

6. It became part of Calais Dentelles, a subsidiary of the Cochez group.

7. Ledieu Beauvillain, Henri and Victor Machu, Robert Belot and Edouard Beauvillain (source: Maison Solstiss).

8. Evening coat, Autumn–Winter 1964–1965 haute couture collection, inv. CiDM 1997.48.4. Photographed by Tom Kublin and published in L'Officiel, nos. 509–510, 1964 (see p. 18 and opposite).

9. Claude Coudray, Marescot's company director at the time, is quoted in L'Officiel, no. 725, 1986, as saying: 'The fact that sequins gained a new lease of life […] was specifically thanks to the demands of Yves Saint Laurent […]'.

ILL. 5 Evening ensemble worn by Maggi Eckardt, Autumn–Winter 1964–1965 haute couture collection. Photograph by Tom Kublin

ILL. 6, P. 96 above 'Soir court' collection board with swatches of Marescot and Dognin lace, Autumn–Winter 1964–1965 haute couture collection.

ILL. 7, P. 96 below 'Soir long' collection board with swatches of Marescot sequinned lace, Autumn–Winter 1984–1985 haute couture collection.

ILL. 8, P. 97 Ensemble worn by Diana Bienvenu, Autumn–Winter 1992–1993 haute couture collection. Hôtel InterContinental, Paris, 29 July 1992. Photograph by Claus Ohm, published in L'Officiel, September 1992.

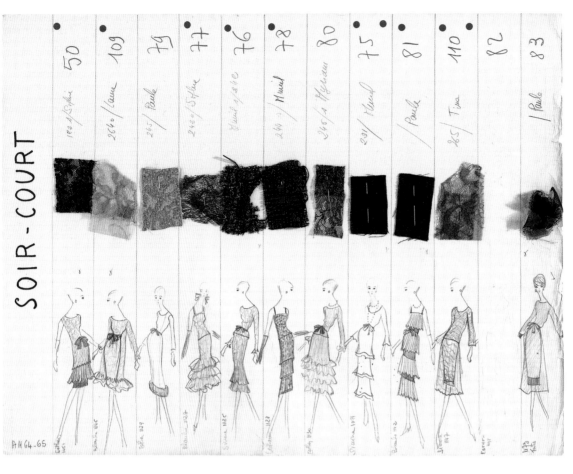

SOIR-COURT

50 109 79 77 76 78 80 75 81 110 82 83

AH 64-65

SOIR LONG

172 162 157 130 174

Marescot

YVESSAINTLAURENT

ILL. 9 Evening gown for the paper doll 'Ivy', 1953–55.

Lace in the Saint Laurent style:
bold and unexpected

Although never dominant, lace was always a feature in Yves Saint Laurent's creations. Way back in 1953, some of the clothes that the young Saint Laurent designed for paper dolls incorporated lace (ILL. 9). Aude Pessey-Lux, who curated an exhibition dedicated to Yves Saint Laurent's use of lace in 2002, noted: '[It] came to dominate his work over the years. A minor presence in the 1960s, it featured more prominently in the 1970s and became indispensable by the 1980s and 1990s.'[10]

Mainly used for evening wear, lace rarely appeared on Yves Saint Laurent's wedding dresses: of his eighty haute couture wedding looks, only seven feature lace.[11] Perhaps he preferred to give this inspirational fabric a less predictable treatment, such as the bold contrast provided by an austere-looking evening dress from his Autumn–Winter 1970–1971 collection with its deeply scooped back veiled in lace,[12] or the sequinned blouses in Chantilly lace that strike such a surprising note beneath the couturier's iconic smoking jackets of 1979 and 1984.[13] The gorgeousness of lace lent itself readily to the playful and suggestive ambiguities of 'under-wear as outerwear': in 1978, lace bras were worn under jackets that were deliberately left unbuttoned, while the cuts and finishes of some dresses, such as those shown for Autumn–Winter 1991–1992, are reminiscent of corsetry (ILL. 10, ILL. 11). SEE P. 78 SEE P. 44

Often lined with silk chiffon, lace suggested what lay beneath, rather than revealing it outright. Saint Laurent's favourite lace was Chantilly – a particularly fine and diaphanous lace, flowing and transparent, which he liked to combine with heavier fabrics. Examples include the blouse (now in Calais) which he teamed with a beige woollen suit[14] (ILL. 12; SEE PP. 114–115) and an evening dress in Darquer lace, belonging to the collections of the Musée Yves Saint Laurent Paris, which was worn beneath a cashmere tuxedo jacket.[15] A boldly patterned black lace could create a striking contrast when overlaid on a coloured fabric ground (ILL. 13) or the lace itself might be in a vivid shade. Embroidered, beaded, sequinned or beribboned, lace could catch the light and create the sort of effects that disguised its nature and left it barely recognizable.

Yves Saint Laurent knew how to exploit the subtleties of lace, and in his hands this delicate openwork fabric took on a life of its own.

10. Aude Pessey-Lux (ed.), *Yves Saint Laurent, 40 ans de création en dentelle*, exhibition catalogue [8 June–29 September 2002], Alençon, Musée des Beaux-Arts et de la Dentelle, 2002.

11. Source: Musée Yves Saint Laurent Paris.

12. Inv. MYSLP HC1970H117.

13. Smoking jacket, Autumn–Winter 1979–1980: inv. MYSLP HC1979H126; tuxedo jacket, Autumn–Winter 1984: inv. MYSLP HC1984H106.

14. Inv. CiDM 1997.48.5 (MYSL HC1981E058), see pp. 114–115.

15. Inv. MYSLP HC1980H055.

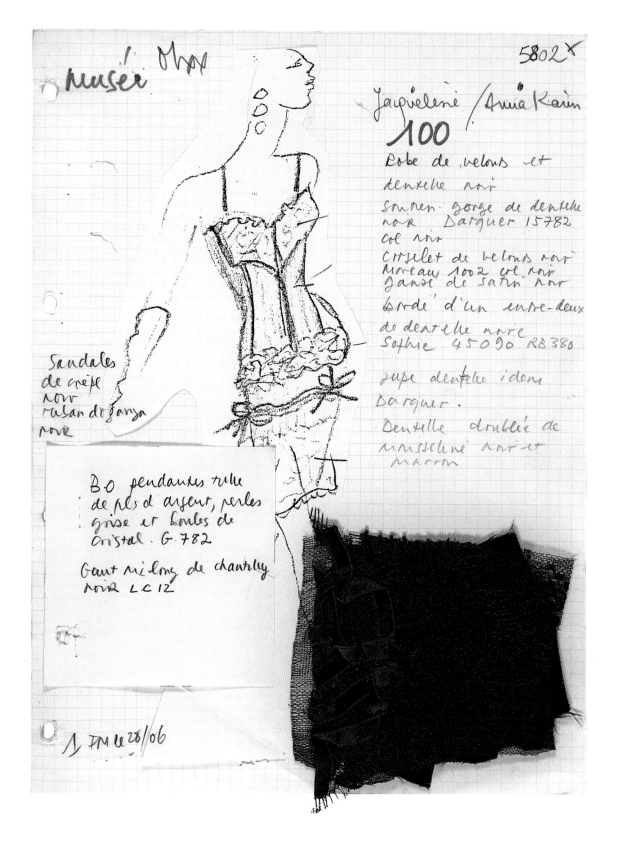

ILL. 10 Atelier specification sheet (or 'Bible page')
for an evening dress in Darquer and Sophie lace,
Autumn–Winter 1991–1992 haute couture collection.

ILL. 11 Evening gown worn by Diana Bienvenu, Autumn–Winter
1991–1992 haute couture collection. Hôtel InterContinental, Paris,
24 July 1991. Photograph by Claus Ohm.

ILL. 12 Suit worn by Kirat Young, Spring–Summer 1981 haute couture collection. Hôtel InterContinental, Paris, 28 January 1981.

ILL. 13 Suit worn by Maureen Gallagher, Autumn–Winter 1990–1991 haute couture collection. Hôtel InterContinental, Paris, 25 July 1990. Photograph by Claus Ohm.

Weaving connections:
from couturier to supplier

Shazia Boucher and Anne-Claire Laronde

YVESSAINTLAURENT   Marescot

Thanks to the exceptional care that the Maison Yves Saint Laurent has always devoted to its archives, the Musée Yves Saint Laurent Paris boasts a remarkable collection of documents, including what were known in-house as 'handling records'. Each handling record refers to a single design and contains information regarding the fabric suppliers, the yardage required, the minimum order quantity and the price. Consequently, we know exactly who supplied the lace for every garment. One name crops up repeatedly: the firm of Marescot. In seeking out the people who run that firm, we were curious to learn more about the couturier's relationship with his lace suppliers.

Bruno Lescroart, a native of Caudry, began his lacemaking career in Calais. In 1985, he took over from his father Étienne as president of the firm of Sophie Hallette, and today his son Romain heads the group, of which the lace manufacturer Riechers-Marescot forms part.

The firm of Marescot mentioned in the Maison Yves Saint Laurent's books was in fact two companies – Riechers and Marescot. The history of Riechers and Marescot is typical of the suppliers of the time, with production and sales being managed independently, as two separate businesses. In the early days, Riechers manufactured 'Calais dress lace'[1] in Calais, while Marescot, located in Paris, took care of sales and distribution. This is why the name of Marescot is the one that regularly appears on the Maison Yves Saint Laurent handling records. In 1986, Riechers bought up Marescot and the two firms were amalgamated under the name Riechers-Marescot.

While it was rare for the Maison's team to visit the manufacturers, the couturier's assistant who looked after deliveries of tulle and lace remained in close contact with the suppliers, who would present their latest designs to the couture house. If there was insufficient stock of the couturier's chosen lace at the showroom, a car would be sent immediately to the factory in Calais. To the textile workers, this way of working may have seemed like rather chaotic. However, the couturier could still be perfecting and adjusting his creations until moments before the start of the collection show, if circumstances allowed. This last-minute timing minimized the risk of anyone copying his designs.

'A collection may be based on an idea that has been utilized before [...] but, for us, it is very important to have direct contact with couturiers and designers. [...] We need to hear their thoughts, their suggestions and their inspirations. Without that contact, we are creating in a vacuum. The fact that sequins gained a new lease of life a few years ago was specifically thanks to demands from Yves Saint Laurent – in 1982, forty-eight designs in his collection featured Riechers-Marescot lace. Every season, we present our selection of lace designs to the couturiers, updated to suit the prevailing trends, and give them sample swatches to help them design their collections. If a couturier falls in love with a fabric, they will place an order. After the collection has been shown, buyers from all over the world will do the same.'[2]

1. 'Dress' means it was designed for use in clothing, as distinct from lingerie.

2. Claude Coudray, marketing manager for the lace manufacturer Riechers-Marescot with responsibility for the French market and relations with haute couture, *L'Officiel de la Mode*, no. 725, 1986, p. 174.

Evening ensemble worn by Dalma Callado, Autumn–Winter 1980–1981 haute couture collection. Photograph by Norman Parkinson, published in *Vogue* Paris, September 1980.

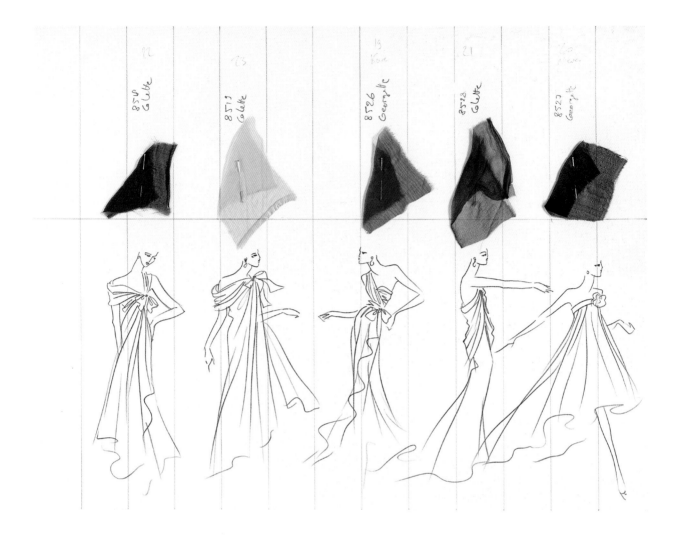

P. 107 Evening dress (detail), Autumn–Winter 1996–1997
haute couture collection. Photograph by Patricia Canino.

ABOVE Collection board, Spring–Summer 2002 haute couture collection.

Sheer fabrics

Cigaline®

Polyamide fabric created by the Lyon manufacturer Bucol. While Cigaline® is as light and sheer as chiffon, the synthetic fibres make it more robust and harder wearing. Its name – taken from the French word *cigale*, meaning 'cicada' – alludes to the insect's diaphanous wings.

Lace

Lace can be either hand- or machine-made and is a fabric composed of solid and open areas; these areas may be transparent or opaque, fine or heavy.

Handmade lace appeared in the first half of the 16th century and was created using either a needle, using a technique similar to embroidery, or bobbins, a craft that was inspired by passementerie or braidmaking.

Machine lace, invented in the 19th century, can include any type of lace, and is produced by either weaving or knitting.

Muslin

Lightweight, transparent cotton or gauze that is extremely soft and flowing. The Italians called it *mossolino* after Mosul, in Iraq, where it was first manufactured.

Organdy

Very lightweight cotton fabric that has been finished to give it a certain stiffness and a crisp feel.

Organza

Sheer silk voile with a light sheen, stiffened and transparent, slightly coarse to the touch, not unlike organdy.

Tulle

Lightweight, transparent fabric produced by twisting threads together to create a circular or polygonal mesh, the dimensions of which vary according to the thickness of the thread that is used. Tulle was once made by hand, with bobbins or needles, but since the 19th century it has been manufactured on mechanical looms.

Glossary

Atelier flou

The atelier responsible for making soft, flowing garments, such as dresses and blouses, from lightweight fabrics such as chiffon and lace.

Atelier specification sheet

Also known as the 'Bible page' (an indication of its importance), the atelier specification sheet was a reproduction of the couturier's original sketch on a perforated sheet of squared paper, to which several fabric samples were pinned. It also listed information about the atelier and the model who would wear the garment, fabric and colour references, the names of suppliers, and the exact accessories that would complete the look.

Atelier tailleur

The atelier responsible for making structured garments, such as coats, jackets and trousers, using stiff materials such as grain de poudre and other woollen fabrics.

Collection board

Collection boards were produced shortly before each runway show. They were stiffened sheets of squared card including reproductions of the original sketches, the names of the ateliers and the models, and production and runway numbers, along with swatches of the textiles used. Sorted according to type of garment, whether day or evening wear, these documents give a complete overview of the collection.

Handling record

Produced by the couture house's stockrooms, the handling record (on cardstock) listed all the textiles and haberdashery required for the creation of a particular look. The list provided precise details of provenance, price and yardage, as well as the total number of hours needed to produce the completed garment.

Manufacturer's advertisement

From the end of the 1970s onwards, exclusive advertising brochures, commissioned by the manufacturers, began to appear in fashion magazines such as *Vogue, Harper's Bazaar* and *L'Officiel*. Made up of a dozen or so glossy pages, they included a series of photographs captioned with the name of the couture house and the name of the textile manufacturer responsible for the fabrics in each design. The photographs might be studio shots or shots taken in the salons at 5 avenue Marceau or in the streets of Paris, or alternatively at one of the collection shows.

Original sketch

The original sketch, made by Yves Saint Laurent and later passed to the *chefs d'atelier*, was the starting point for the creation of a garment in the atelier.

Polaroid

When a garment was completed, Polaroid snapshots were taken so that the couturier could then decide which accessories were required. The Polaroid was a working document, and as such it carried the name of the collection, the production number, the name of the model and her runway number.

Press pack photograph

Commissioned by the couture house, these photographs were taken a few days before or after each runway show and required confidentiality on the part of the photographer until the new collection was revealed to the press. They were posed photographs, shot inside or outside the couture house or in the photographer's studio. They were assembled into press packs or arranged in albums used to showcase the designs for clients or foreign buyers.

Atelier specification sheet for an evening gown,
Autumn–Winter 1996–1997 haute couture collection.

Research sketch

Drawn by Yves Saint Laurent for his collection, the research sketch, or 'unselected sketch', did not lead to the creation of a garment. It might be a sketch for a silhouette finalized in an original sketch, or a design that was either not selected or abandoned midway through the creative process.

Runway photograph

These photographs were taken on behalf of the couture house once a collection show was under way, and showed each look being modelled in front of an audience. Between 1962 and 1976, runway shows took place in the salons at the Maison, and in later years in the Salon Impérial of the Hôtel InterContinental, on the rue de Castiglione, Paris. Taken by freelance photographers who worked regularly for the Maison, these photographs played a key role in advertising and selling a new collection.

Toile

A prototype version of a garment made from unbleached cotton, the toile is the first rendering of a design in three-dimensional form. Details such as buttons and pockets are drawn on in charcoal.

Yves Saint Laurent: A brief chronology

1936

Yves Mathieu-Saint-Laurent is born in Oran, Algeria, on 1 August. While still in his teens, he designs two fashion collections for paper dolls, for Autumn–Winter 1953 and 1954, as well as a number of stage costumes and theatre sets.

1954

Leaves for Paris after winning third prize in a competition organized by the Secrétariat International de la Laine.

1955

Spends a few months studying at the École de la Chambre Syndicale de la Haute Couture in Paris (ECSCP). Michel de Brunhoff, editor-in-chief at *Vogue* Paris, introduces Saint Laurent to Christian Dior, who takes him on as his assistant.

1957

Takes over as artistic director of Maison Dior after the death of Christian Dior (1905–57). His first collection, the 'Ligne Trapèze' or Trapeze Line, shown in January 1958, is a phenomenal success.

1958

Meets Pierre Bergé (1930–2017). The two men become life partners and business partners – a relationship that will continue until the couturier's death.

1959

Produces his first designs for the ballet *Cyrano de Bergerac*, choreographed by Roland Petit. A great many designs for ballet, stage and cinema will follow.

1961

The Maison Yves Saint Laurent opens in December in Paris, at 30*bis* rue Spontini.

1962

Shows his first collection on 29 January. The 1960s become a decade of iconic Yves Saint Laurent creations, including the peacoat (1962), the Mondrian dress (1965), the tuxedo (1966), the Pop Art dress (1966), the jumpsuit (1968) and the safari jacket (1968).

1966

Creates his first sheer designs. The 'nude look' is born in 1968, with blouses in Cigaline® that reveal the wearer's breasts and a chiffon dress that reveals the entire body.

Saint Laurent discovers Marrakesh, a city that will profoundly influence his work and where he will design many of his collections.

Launch of the SAINT LAURENT *rive gauche* ready-to-wear line and the opening of his first store, on the rue de Tournon in Paris.

1970

Shows his dress with the plunge back in Chantilly lace at the Autumn–Winter haute couture runway show. The dress is immortalized in a photograph by Jeanloup Sieff.

1974

The Maison Yves Saint Laurent moves to 5 avenue Marceau, Paris.

1983

The exhibition at the Metropolitan Museum of Art in New York, *Yves Saint Laurent: 25 Years of Design*, is the first exhibition dedicated to the couturier during his lifetime.

Yves Saint Laurent in his studio at 5 avenue Marceau, Paris, 1978.
Photograph by Patrice Habans.

Others will follow worldwide –
in Beijing, Moscow, Sydney,
Tokyo and again in Paris.

2002

The Maison Yves Saint Laurent
closes. A retrospective show
at the Centre Pompidou looks
at forty years of creativity,
as represented by over three
hundred looks. The Fondation
Pierre Bergé – Yves Saint
Laurent is founded and, in
2004, opens at 5 avenue
Marceau with the exhibition
*Yves Saint Laurent, dialogue
avec l'art*. Between 2004
and 2016, more than twenty
exhibitions follow, devoted
to art, fashion and design.

2008

Yves Saint Laurent dies on
1 June, aged seventy-one.

2017

Pierre Bergé dies at the age of
eighty-six. The two Yves Saint
Laurent museums open, in
Paris and Marrakesh.

2022

An anniversary show, *Yves Saint
Laurent aux musées*, is held at
six Paris museums: the Centre
Pompidou, the Musée d'Art
Moderne de Paris, the Louvre,
the Musée d'Orsay, the Musée
National Picasso and the Musée
Yves Saint Laurent Paris.

Bibliography

MONOGRAPHS

Laurence Benaïm, *Yves Saint Laurent: A Biography*, New York: Rizzoli, 2019

Béatrice Dupire and Hady Sy (ed.), *Yves Saint Laurent: Forty Years of Creation*, New York: International Festival of Fashion Photography, 1998

Marguerite Duras, *Yves Saint Laurent et la photographie de mode*, Paris: Albin Michel, 1988

Olivier Flaviano, Aurélie Samuel, Suzy Menkes, Jéromine Savignon, *Yves Saint Laurent Catwalk*, London: Thames & Hudson, 2019

Fondation Pierre Bergé – Yves Saint Laurent, Pierre Bergé (foreword), *Yves Saint Laurent, haute couture. L'oeuvre intégral, 1962–2002*, Paris: Éditions de La Martinière, 2010

Catherine Ormen, *All About Yves*, London: Laurence King, 2017

Aurélie Samuel (ed.), *Les musées Yves Saint Laurent Paris/Marrakech*, Paris: RMB, 2017

Jéromine Savignon, *Yves Saint Laurent's Studio: Mirror and Secrets*, Arles: Actes Sud, 2014

David Teboul, *Yves Saint Laurent, 5, avenue Marceau, 75116 Paris, France*, New York: H.N. Abrams, 2002

EXHIBITION CATALOGUES

Diana Vreeland (ed.), *Yves Saint Laurent: 25 Years of Design*, exhibition catalogue [New York: Metropolitan Museum of Art, 14 December 1983–2 September 1984], New York: Clarkson N. Potter, 1983

Yves Saint Laurent, Hélène De Turckheim, Bernard-Henri Lévy (foreword), *Yves Saint Laurent par Yves Saint Laurent*, exhibition catalogue [Paris: Musée des Arts de la Mode, 30 May–26 October 1986], Paris: Editions Herscher, 1986

Aude Pessey-Lux (ed.), *Yves Saint Laurent: 40 ans de création en dentelle*, exhibition catalogue [Alençon: Musée des Beaux-Arts et de la Dentelle, 8 June–29 September 2002], Alençon: Musée des Beaux-Arts et de la Dentelle, 2002 Fondation Pierre Bergé – Yves Saint Laurent, Dominique Païni

(foreword), *Yves Saint Laurent: Dialogue avec l'art*, exhibition catalogue [Paris: Fondation Pierre Bergé – Yves Saint Laurent, 10 March–31 October 2004], Paris: Fondation Pierre Bergé – Yves Saint Laurent, 2004

Florence Müller, Farid Chenoune, *Yves Saint Laurent*, exhibition catalogue [Paris: Musée du Petit Palais, 11 March–29 August 2010], Paris: Éditions de La Martinière, 2010; English ed.: New York, Abrams, 2010

Olivier Saillard, Alexandre Samson, Dominique Veillon, *Yves Saint Laurent, 1971: La collection du scandale*, exhibition catalogue [Paris: Fondation Pierre Bergé – Yves Saint Laurent, 19 March–19 July 2015], Paris: Flammarion/Fondation Pierre Bergé – Yves Saint Laurent, 2015; English ed.: New York: Abrams, 2017

Sylvie Marot (ed.), *Haute dentelle*, exhibition catalogue [Calais: Cité de la Dentelle et de la Mode, 9 June 2018–6 January 2019], Ghent: Snoeck, 2018

Alexandre Samson (ed.), *Back Side / Dos à la mode*, exhibition catalogue [Paris: Musée Bourdelle, 5 July–17 November 2019], Paris: Paris Musées, 2019

Aurélie Samuel, Esclarmonde Monteil (eds.), *Yves Saint Laurent: les coulisses de la haute couture à Lyon*, exhibition catalogue [Lyon: Musée des Tissus, 9 November 2019–8 March 2020; Paris: Musée Yves Saint Laurent Paris, 17 June 2022–5 December 2021], Paris: Musée Yves Saint Laurent; Lyon: Libel, 2019

OTHER WORKS

Christopher Breward, 'Couture as queer auto/biography', in Valerie Steele (ed.), *A Queer History of Fashion: From the Closet to the Catwalk*, New Haven: Yale University Press, 2013

Antoine De Baecque, 'Écrans. Le corps au cinéma', in Jean-Jacques Courtine (ed.), *Histoire du corps*, vol. 3: *Les mutations du regard, le XXe siècle*, Paris: Seuil, 2005, pp. 371–390

Claude Fauque, *Les mots du textile*, Paris: Belin, 2013

Martine Fosse (ed.), *Galeries des collections*, Calais: Cité de la Dentelle et de la Mode, 2010

Anne Hollander, *Seeing Through Clothes*, New York: Viking Press, 1978

Lydia Kamitsis, *Dentelle de Calais-Caudry – l'art de tisser le rêve*, Paris: Lienart, 2021

James Laver, *Modesty in Dress: An Inquiry Into the Fundamentals of Fashion*, Boston: Houghton Mifflin, 1969

Laura Mulvey, 'Visual pleasure and narrative cinema' (1973), in *Visual and Other Pleasures*, London: Palgrave Macmillan, 1989

Nancy Troy, *Couture Culture: A Study of Modern Art and Fashion*, Cambridge, MA: MIT Press, 2003.

ARTICLES

Deirdre McSharry, 'Eves, St. Laurent', *The Sun*, 30 January 1968

Felicity Green, 'Sex hits Paris for six', *Daily Mirror*, 24 February 1968

Simone Baron, Françoise Quilici, 'La Mode. Il ne faut pas enlever la veste', *France-Soir – Paris-Presse, L'Intransigeant*, 26 February 1968

Françoise Sagan, 'Saint Laurent par Françoise Sagan', *Elle* (France), 3 March 1980

Yvonne Baby, 'Yves Saint Laurent au Metropolitan de New York. Portrait de l'artiste', *Le Monde*, 8 December 1983

Claude Coudray, 'Riechers-Marescot, la création en dentelle', *L'Officiel de la Mode*, no. 725, 1986

Catherine Deneuve, 'SAINT LAURENT, le magnifique', *Globe* (France), 1 May 1986

Khemais Ben Lakhdar Rezgui, 'Automne–hiver 1968 chez Yves Saint Laurent, La transparence scandaleuse d'une robe du soir', *Pièce détachée*, vol. 1: *La Robe*, 1 November 2018

PP. 114–115 Suit blouse (detail), Spring–Summer 1981 haute couture collection. Cité de la Dentelle et de la Mode collection, Calais. Photograph by Patricia Canino.

P. 116 Blouse (detail), part of an evening ensemble, Autumn–Winter 1979–1980 haute couture collection. Photograph by Patricia Canino.

This book was published on the occasion of the exhibition *Yves Saint Laurent: Transparences*, jointly organized by the Cité de la Dentelle et de la Mode, Calais, and the Musée Yves Saint Laurent Paris, and presented in two phases: Phase 1 at the Cité de la Dentelle et de la Mode, Calais, from 24 June to 12 November 2023; Phase 2 at the Musée Yves Saint Laurent Paris, from 9 February to 1 September 2024.

GENERAL DIRECTORS
(PHASE 1)
Elsa Janssen,
director of the Musée Yves Saint Laurent Paris
Anne-Claire Laronde,
head curator,
director of Musées de la Ville de Calais

SCIENTIFIC DIRECTORS
(PHASE 1)
Shazia Boucher,
senior curator, deputy director of the Musées de la Ville de Calais
Domitille Éblé,
curator, head of graphic art collections for the Musée Yves Saint Laurent Paris

SCIENTIFIC COMMITTEE
(PHASE 1)
Serena Bucalo-Mussely,
curator, head of collections for the Musée Yves Saint Laurent Paris
Alice Coulon-Saillard,
curator, head of photography, audiovisual and press archive collections for the Musée Yves Saint Laurent Paris
Sophie Henwood,
associate curator, head of collections for the Musées de la Ville de Calais
Judith Lamas,
curator, head of textiles and accessories collections for the Musée Yves Saint Laurent Paris

EXHIBITION DESIGN (PHASE 1)
Studio Tovar: Simon de Tovar and Alain Batifoulier

The exhibition in Calais benefits from the support of the Direction Régionale des Affaires Culturelles Hauts-de-France, the Conseil Départemental du Pas-de-Calais and the Amis des Musées de Calais.

CITY OF CALAIS

Natacha Bouchart,
mayor of Calais, president of Grand Calais, Terres & Mers, and vice-president of the Hauts-de-France region
Pascal Pestre,
deputy director for tourism, vice-president of Grand Calais, Terres & Mers
Vincent Leray,
general director of services
Antoine Foissey,
deputy general director for tourism
Pascal Foschi,
culture and community director

CITÉ DE LA DENTELLE ET DE LA MODE

DIRECTORS
Anne-Claire Laronde,
head curator, museum director
Shazia Boucher,
senior curator, museum deputy director

EXHIBITIONS AND DOCUMENTATION DEPARTMENT
Shazia Boucher,
senior curator, museum deputy director, head of exhibitions department
Marie-Astrid Hennart, Anthony Cadet

COLLECTIONS DEPARTMENT
Sophie Henwood,
associate curator, head of collections
Stéphane Capon, Peggy Charles, Natacha Haffringues, Maud Malet-Grondin, intern

VISITOR MANAGEMENT DEPARTMENT
Delphine Nicola,
associate curator, head of visitor management
Sylvie Brismalin, Caroline Duquenoy, Michel Friant, Victorien Garenaux, Nathalie Jung, Gilles Lavie, Julie Parenty, Christophe Quenette, Pierre Weymeesch, Diane Maussire, intern

COMMUNICATIONS
Maïté Parenty,
head of communications
Sophie Rose

MUSEUM GUIDES
Élisabeth Calais, Marie-Laure Dumont-Fourmanoir, Myriam Hamelin, Jean Marmier, Émilie Questroy, Fabien Questroy, Fabien Rock

ADMINISTRATION
Isabelle Dhaussy,
head of administration and finance
Christine Bosc, Anouchka Chappé, Linda Hamlaoui

VISITOR RELATIONS
Grégory Hélie,
head of visitor relations
Louisa Benaidji, Sonia Bouchez, Nathalie Boulanger, Lydia Corion, Gaëlle Chaubert, Olivier Dewet, Cynthia Dubuis, Zohra Duvivier, Dorothée Fournier, François Guilmain, Vincent Mele, Hélène Mouchon, Nathalie Ragot, Isabelle Roche

TECHNICAL AND MAINTENANCE DEPARTMENT
Frédéric Merveillie, technical manager
Éric Boulanger, Manuel Castelle, Daniel Gest, Anita Levaillant, Sylvain Popiol, Gaston Pruvot, Aline Sauvage, Jérôme Tissandier

Acknowledgments

We would like to thank the City of Calais, as represented by Natacha Bouchart, Mayor of Calais, President of the Grand Calais Terres & Mers community and Vice-President of the Région Hauts-de-France, and Pascal Pestre, Deputy Mayor and Vice-President of the Grand Calais Terres & Mers community, for the confidence they have placed in this project.

We would also like to thank Madison Cox, President of the Fondation Pierre Bergé – Yves Saint Laurent, Elsa Janssen, Director, and Domitille Éblé, Curator of the Musée Yves Saint Laurent Paris, together with Anne-Claire Laronde, Chief Heritage Curator and Director, and Shazia Boucher, Heritage Curator and Deputy Director of the Musées de la Ville de Calais, for their support and collaboration at every stage of this exhibition relating to the use of transparency in the work of Yves Saint Laurent.

We wish to express our gratitude to Olivier Flaviano, Aurélie Samuel and Lola Fournier for initiating this joint project between the two museums, and also to Leslie Veyrat and Sylvie Marot for their contribution to the birth of the project.

Our thanks also go to the photographer Patricia Canino, who brought her unique vision to bear on Yves Saint Laurent's sheer designs throughout the photoshoots for this book and the Calais exhibition; to Émilie Hammen, art and fashion historian and lecturer at the Institut Français de la Mode, for her reflections on 'The body laid bare by the couturier', and to Agnès Dahan, who oversaw the design for this book.

It was a pleasure to talk to the model Rebecca Ayoko and lace manufacturer Bruno Lescroart, both of whom helped to make this book richer.

We wish to extend our deepest gratitude to all the staff at both institutions for helping to get this exhibition off the ground and make it a success. To all our partners and all those involved in this project at both the Cité de la Dentelle et de la Mode and the Musée Yves Saint Laurent Paris, please accept our sincere thanks for your contribution to the project's success.

The Cité de la Dentelle et de la Mode would like to pay a special tribute to Manuel Castelle, a member of the technical team who died suddenly in March 2023.

Cité de la Dentelle et de la Mode and Musée Yves Saint Laurent Paris

Picture credits

Translated from the French *Yves Saint Laurent: Transparences* by Ruth Sharman

First published in the United Kingdom in 2024
by Thames & Hudson Ltd, 181A High Holborn,
London WC1V 7QX

First published in the United States of America
in 2024 by Thames & Hudson Inc., 500 Fifth Avenue,
New York, New York 10110

British Library Cataloguing-in-Publication Data
A catalogue record for this book is available from
the British Library

Library of Congress Catalog Card Number
2023948720

ISBN 978-0-500-02800-1

Printed and bound in Italy by L.E.G.O. Spa

Be the first to know about our new releases,
exclusive content and author events by visiting
thamesandhudson.com
thamesandhudsonusa.com
thamesandhudson.com.au

PP. 122–128 Evening gown (detail), Spring–Summer 1978
haute couture collection; tuxedo jacket (detail), SAINT LAURENT
rive gauche collection, Cité de la Dentelle et de la Mode
collection, Calais; evening gown (detail), Autumn–Winter
1991–1992 haute couture collection; evening gown (detail),
Autumn–Winter 1991–1992 haute couture collection.
Photographs by Patricia Canino.

BACK COVER Evening gown (detail), Spring–Summer 1975
haute couture collection. Photograph by Patricia Canino.

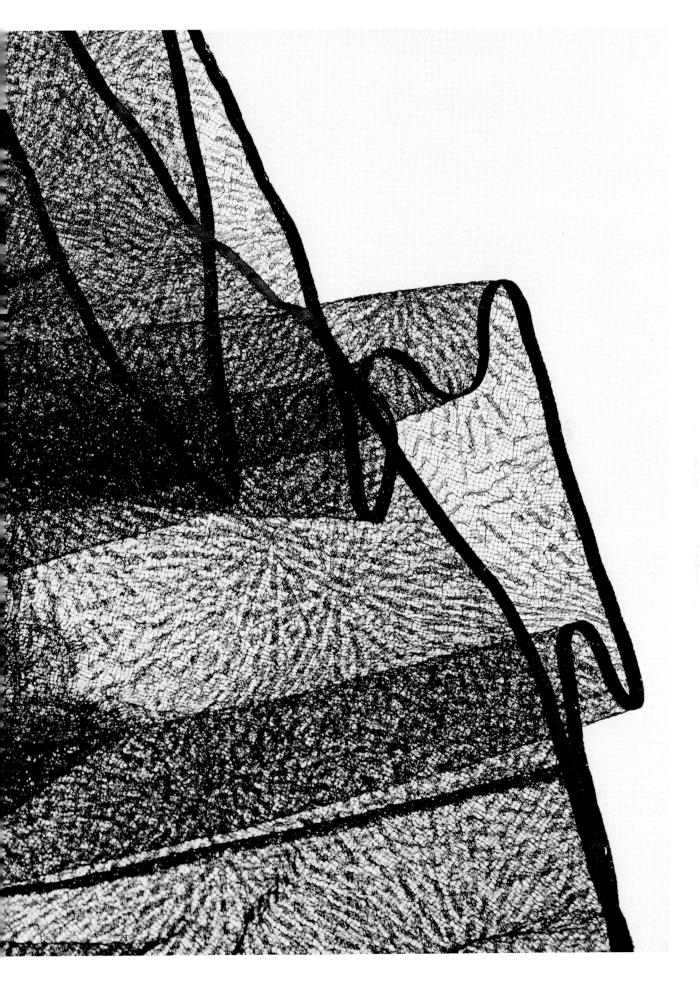

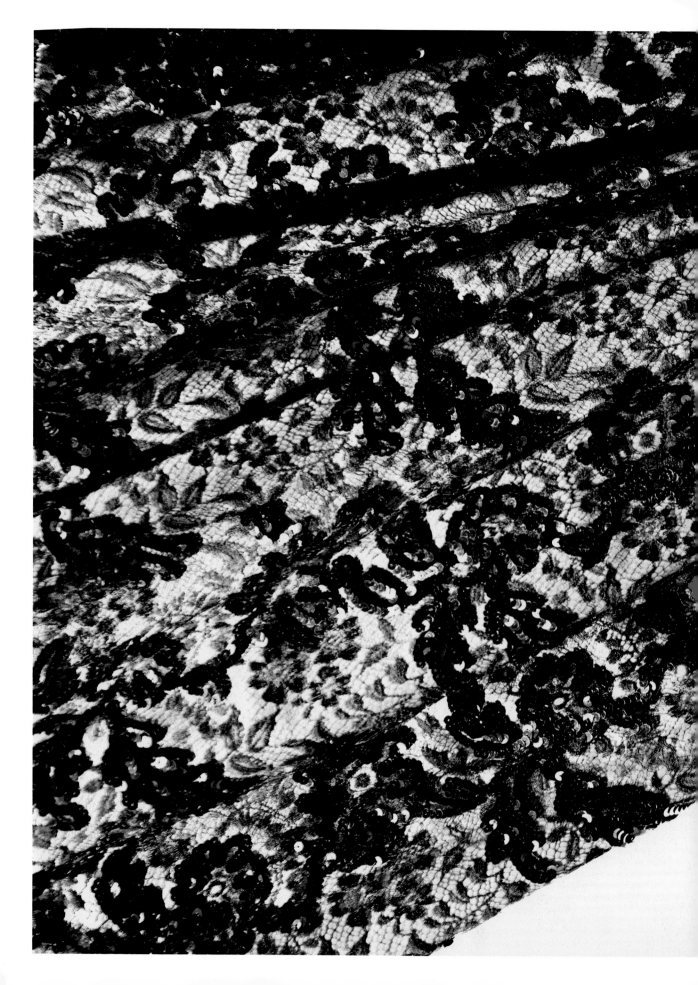

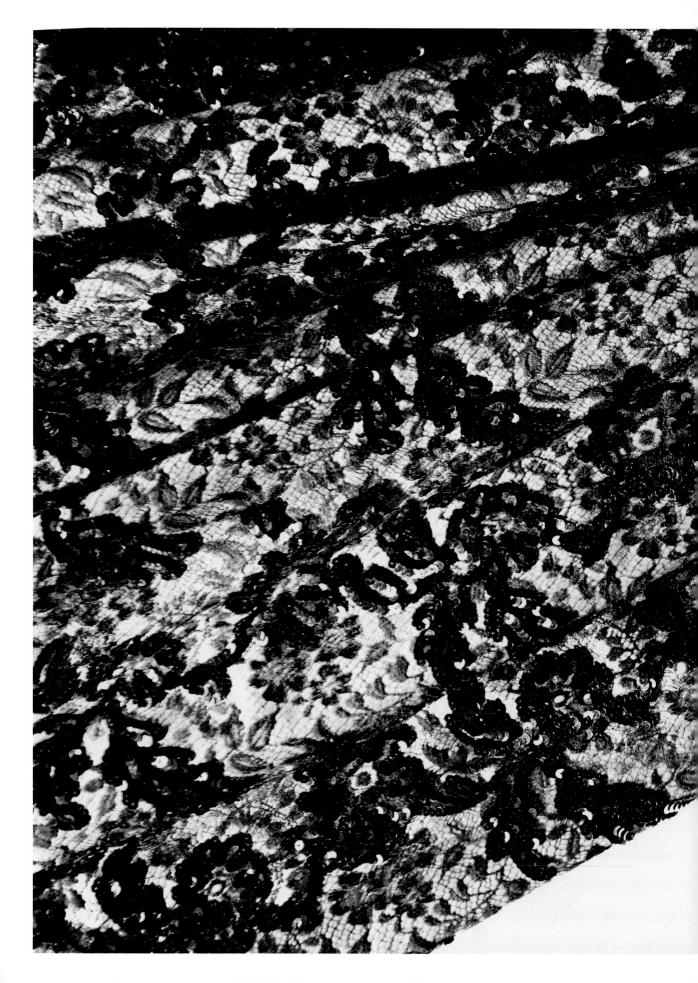